Sir Edmund Bacon

A NORFOLK LIFE

Sir Edmund Castell Bacon ('Mindy'):
a portrait by Alan Gwynne-Jones, 1969

Sir Edmund Bacon

A NORFOLK LIFE

BY

DONALD LINDSAY

with a foreword by
BAMBER GASCOIGNE

THE PLUME PRESS

1988

First published in 1988
by the Plume Press Ltd
West Bowers Hall, Woodham Walter
Maldon, Essex CM9 6RZ
Printed and bound in Great Britain by
Butler & Tanner Ltd, Frome and London

ISBN 0 947 65601 4

British Library Cataloguing in Publication Data

Lindsay, Donald, *1910–*
    Sir Edmund Bacon: a Norfolk life.
    1. Norfolk. Social life, 1901–
    Biographies
    I. Title
    942.6'1082'0924

Contents

FOR

PRISCILLA

Illustrations

FIGURES IN THE TEXT

Foreword

It was my great good fortune to have Mindy as a godfather. I cannot, admittedly, remember him taking me very often through my catechism. The advantages were rather different. Through him I seemed to come into contact with a living example of an English country gentleman in the superb tradition of the eighteenth century, the heyday of the English countryside, when owners of great estates were fascinated by art and architecture, and when the best of them represented the new breed of 'improving' landlords (the most famous of them all being also a local man, Coke of Norfolk).

This had been no more than my personal impression of Mindy's qualities, but it is amply confirmed on the broader canvas of Donald Lindsay's excellent biography. So many details fit the pattern. The intense involvement with the Territorials, starting early on between the wars, is part of an age-old English tradition, though two centuries ago it would have been muskets to stop the French rather than anti-tank guns against the Germans.

The same is true of all Mindy's work after the war for East Anglia's university and for Norwich's great cathedral, symbolized perhaps above all in his superbly imaginative idea in getting Norfolk landowners each to fell a great oak for the timbers of the roof; 'hearts of oak are our men', they had sung that first in the eighteenth century. And then all those years of representing the monarch as Lord Lieutenant of the county; and the regular trips to Windsor for the Garter ceremony; and the stream of connoisseurs coming to Raveningham to look at the paintings; and the little matter of looking after Sir Nicholas Bacon's two fields in the city of London.

It was not that Mindy was old-fashioned — merely that his life was shot through in the most enviable way with the threads of English history, and even more specifically with those of Bacon history in Norfolk. But few, even given his advantages, contrive to weave such a full new chapter of their own.

The amazing variety of his life reached me only through the amazing variety of guests round the dining-room table. Here people of all sorts, from clerics to art historians, from judges to tycoons, always with a healthy leavening of old or local friends, would sit down in an atmosphere of informality which often teetered enjoyably on the verge of chaos.

The show was invariably kept on the road by the warmth of Priscilla's welcome, by the eagerness of Mindy to engage in energetic conversation on an enormous range of topics, and by an undercurrent of amused anarchy injected by any of their children who might be staying. The upshot was that nothing seemed to matter and every such occasion was exhilarating and immensely enjoyable.

I think it was on my very last visit to Raveningham, just a few weeks before Mindy died, that the fruit salad had been rather trendily served in four large scooped out pineapples. Unfortunately the four principal guests, served first, took a pineapple each. Somehow Mindy was able to make it seem that the other twelve of us had actually chosen cheese.

How pleased Mindy would be, with his sense of continuity, to see the state of affairs at Raveningham now, with Nicholas and Susie and their children living in the house. I well remember the excitement in May 1953 when news came of Nicholas's birth (an excitement increased for me when Mindy made his own godson, still at Eton, his son's godfather). After four daughters the premier baronetcy was at last safe for another generation, though I must say that there was never the slightest impression that any of the daughters were regarded as 'disappointments', as Donald Lindsay relates of their four aunts. Mindy lived to see Nicholas and Susie married, but died two years before the birth of their first son.

I am certain that Mindy would have enjoyed this book but am equally sure that he would never have let on. I can just imagine him putting it down after a first reading, with something between a grunt and a 'humph', and the remark: 'Allright, I suppose, if you like that kind of thing.'

BAMBER GASCOIGNE

Preface

I only had the privilege of knowing Sir Edmund Bacon for a very short while towards the end of his life. He had helped me with information about Bishop Launcelot Fleming, an account of whose career the Bishop's wife had asked me to write, and Sir Edmund kindly agreed to write a foreword to the book. In March 1986 I unexpectedly received a letter from Priscilla Lady Bacon asking if I would be prepared 'to do for Mindy what you did for Launcelot'. I accepted her trusting invitation and this memoir is the result.

In writing the book I was to a very large extent dependent upon the readiness of those who had known him well to tell me about him. Priscilla was the chief source of evidence and I cannot be sufficiently grateful for her readiness to answer all my questions and her insistence that I should be critical of him if I so wished. Her son, Nicholas, and his four sisters have all helped me to see him as he was when, so to speak, off-duty. In all, over one hundred people have spoken or written to me about him. I trust that I may be allowed to thank them all most sincerely without mentioning each by name. I must, however, thank Bamber Gascoigne, Mindy's godson and godfather to Nicholas, for sparing time in a busy life to read the typescript and write the foreword.

It is inevitable that many may question what I have said about Mindy at certain points in his career. All that I would hope is that this memoir will keep alive in the minds of family and friends the memory of a devoted servant of Norfolk and at the same time a humble and much-loved man.

DONALD LINDSAY

Seaford 1986–88

1

Family Tree

'About a century and a half ago it was fashionable for families to have their pedigrees prepared, going back into the dim ages. I have a suspicion that my family did the same thing.' So wrote the subject of this book, Sir Edmund Bacon, in reply to one of many seeking information about the Bacon pedigree, at times half-hoping to claim kinship. Since there are a great number of Edmund Bacons on the family tree – for the Christian names bestowed on eldest sons, Edmund or Nicholas, remain largely unchanged over the centuries – it will be simpler for the purposes of this account of his life to use the affectionate nickname 'Mindy' by which he was always known to his host of friends.

Inability to obtain incontrovertible evidence about his family in earliest times did not discourage Mindy from taking a keen interest in his ancestry. He maintained that many family pedigrees needed to be taken with more than a grain of salt and his matter-of-fact approach to the subject made him guess that 'it is more likely that we originated from fair-haired, blue-eyed Saxon pirates', some of whom settled at Hessett in Suffolk, between Bury St Edmunds and Stowmarket, which is 'where we sprang from originally'. He regretted that so few of his forebears seem to have shared his interest in the long story of the Bacon family. 'The trouble with my family has been that although they have always lived in East Anglia they were prone to move about in the most extraordinary way. Not only that, but when they left one house or estate they seem to have picked up a hat, walked out of the door and left all the contents intact to the new purchaser. My own view is that the family prospered in very early days – the

Gorleston church brass, for instance – then I think fell on evil days, until they came back through Sir Nicholas Bacon, the Lord Keeper, in the late 16th century. But I have no proof of this.'

Nicholas Bacon, son of a Suffolk yeoman farmer, was born in 1509 and was probably educated at the Abbey school in Bury before entering Corpus Christi College, Cambridge, at the age of thirteen. Corpus was a college which became closely associated with the Bacon family and after four years there Nicholas in his final examination was placed third in the whole university. After a short period of travel in France he studied law at Gray's Inn and gradually became known as a rising lawyer, involved in the affairs of the Inn and solicitor to Cambridge University. It was at Cambridge that he became a close friend of Willam Cecil, later Lord Burghley, and the two men were to rise together from comparative obscurity to positions of authority. This they were to achieve by their own efforts and by keeping a prudent watch over the rapidly changing turn of events in the mid-sixteenth century.

When between 1529 and 1536 Henry VIII dissolved the monasteries, Bacon hoped that part of the appropriated wealth would be devoted to setting up a college for the education of future statesmen. This was a wise and far-seeing suggestion at a time when laymen were rapidly replacing the clergy, hitherto almost the only educated body of men, in the higher administrative and diplomatic posts. Nothing came of his suggestion. Instead, he personally gained by inheriting large estates previously held by the monasteries of St Albans, Walsingham, Thetford and Bury St Edmunds. As a staunch Protestant he came to favour during the brief reign of Edward VI but his religious beliefs placed him in potential danger on the accession of the Catholic Queen Mary. In the turmoil following Edward's death and the attempt to make Lady Jane Grey Queen he wisely withdrew to his Suffolk mansion at Redgrave to await events. As a lawyer he believed that he should uphold Mary's legitimate claim to the throne; as a Protestant he deplored at her Catholic faith: the lawyer won and he offered the Queen his loyal services, thereby possibly saving himself from the headsman's axe. However, he played no part in public life during her reign but managed his estate and occupied himself profitably as a sheep farmer.

Agas's woodcut map of London, *c.* 1560 which includes the two fields given by Elizabeth I to Sir Nicholas Bacon in gratitude for his services and which have belonged to the Bacon family since that time

It was with the accession of Queen Elizabeth in 1558 that his political career began. He at once became a Secretary of State and on 22 December of that year the Queen appointed him Lord Keeper of the Privy Seal and knighted him. At first both he and Cecil had much to do with ecclesiastical affairs, which were largely entrusted to them. In 1559 he was given the full authority of a Lord Chancellor and became increasingly concerned with the threat to Queen and country from the activities of Mary, Queen of Scots. His balanced political opinions came from honest conviction and he was able to express them with fluency and a directness of speech, spiced with a cheery good humour, earning the tribute of being 'an archpiece of wit and wisdom'.

This first Sir Nicholas Bacon had in 1550 purchased the estate of Gorhambury in Hertfordshire, where in 1563 he began to build the famous house, completed after six years at a cost of £1,894.11s.9d, a considerable sum at the time. Over the entrance he inscribed the family motto, *Mediocria Firma*, 'Moderation is Stable' (or endures), well-suited to one noted for his wise and judicious advice. He had once acted as host to his sovereign at Redgrave where Elizabeth had commented: 'My Lord, what a little house you have gotten.' This provoked one of Nicholas's famous repartees: 'Madam, my house is well, but it is you who have made me too great for my house.' At Gorhambury he twice had to entertain the Queen and her enormous retinue, visitations enjoyed by her as a method of economy while sometimes nearly bankrupting her loyal subjects. For the second occasion in 1577 Nicholas built a new gallery and the six-day visit cost him about one-fifth of the entire cost of the building. To show her gratitude for the services which her Lord Keeper had rendered Queen Elizabeth presented him with two fields within the City of London on which to graze his cattle – doubtless a convenience at the time but an invaluable financial asset four centuries later.

Nicholas married twice. His first wife, Jane, daughter of William Fernley of West Creting in Suffolk, bore him three sons and three daughters. She was never strong and was content to hand over much of the care of her family to Ann, daughter of Sir Anthony Cooke, tutor to Edward VI. Child-bearing proved too great a strain on her and she died. Shortly after her death Nicholas married Ann, a formidable blue-stocking, who read Latin, Greek,

A portrait of Sir Nicholas Bacon, knight, 1510–1579, Lord Keeper,
which has always been in the family

Italian and French 'as her native tongue', and a puritanically religious woman. It was she who was mother to Anthony, diplomat and friend of the ill-fated Earl of Essex and to the famous Francis Bacon, Lord High Chancellor, philosopher and writer, the Renaissance man who 'took all knowledge for his province'. Many still believe that Mindy was a direct descendant of this brilliant if controversial man but this he always stoutly denied. Once in the United States he met a man 'who came enthusiastically up to me and said: "Is your name Bacon?" and I said "yes" and he said "So is mine, shake hands". Then he went on to say that he was a direct descendant of Francis Bacon and I said "You had much better not be because he never had any legitimate children".' Mindy always looked to the Lord Keeper as the founder of his family and when designing his own bookplate he copied that of his ancestor.

As the years went by Nicholas became, in Camden's phrase, 'exceedingly gross-bodied'. He took little exercise and suffered agonies of pain from gout and also from 'the stone'. He realized that his life was drawing to its close and he obtained permission from the Dean to start erecting his tomb in St Paul's Cathedral. He showed great courage on bearing his many afflictions, sitting for two hours at a time in a bath filled with water, milk and herbs, but on 20 February 1579 he died in his official London residence, York Place near Charing Cross. His death was said to have resulted from the timidity of his barber, who allowed him to fall asleep with a cold draught blowing full upon him and feared to wake him. York House was draped in black, as was much of the Cathedral, on the day of the elaborate funeral procession and service. His tomb, like almost everything else in the Cathedral, was destroyed in the Great Fire of 1666. His stone torso, minus the legs, survived and is today in the crypt of the re-built St Paul's. 400 years after his death, Mindy and some of the family attended a service in his memory in the Cathedral and a further service of re-dedication was held in 1982 when the crypt was restored and refurbished.

A portrait of the Lord Keeper, painted in the last year of his life, and a terra-cotta bust, both at Gorhambury, show, in every sense, a man of weight, impressively firm and decisive. Four centuries later Mindy possessed many of the characteristics of his great ancestor – shrewd powers of judgement, a strong sense of public service, considerable ability as a speaker and a love of good stories. These characteristics could not over such a long span of years be described as being inherited but in a curious throwback Mindy in later life developed the Tudor cast of countenance so familiar from the drawings of Holbein.

Nicholas was succeeded by the eldest son of his first marriage, also called Nicholas, who lived at Redgrave. Like his father he had entered Gray's Inn before turning to politics, becoming member for Beverley in 1562 and then for his county of Suffolk from 1572 until 1583. He was knighted in the year before his father died and three years later became High Sheriff of Suffolk. Before he died the Lord Keeper had set up his second son, Nathaniel, in the estate at Stiffkey in Norfolk, where he ruled the north of the county with a rod of iron. The first volume of Nathaniel's collected papers, an important record of Tudor local history, was presented to Mindy in 1979 shortly after he had retired from being Lord Lieutenant of Norfolk.

It soon became clear that the death of Queen Elizabeth in 1603 and the accession of James I from Scotland would in no way halt the advance of the Bacon family. The Stuarts were always chronically short of money; to a large extent this was due to rapid inflation resulting from the flow of silver into Europe from the Spanish possessions in the New World and minted to pay the Spanish troops. This coincided with the rising power of parliament, ignorant of economic forces beyond its control, and determined to gain an increasing share in the business of government in return for grudgingly voting supplies. By 1611 James's financial straits drove him to institute by letters patent 'a new dignitie between Barons and Knights', to be neither a part of the peerage nor an order of knighthood. Because the money needed by James was ostensibly for the support of troops, for whose pay the Crown was still responsible, those to be created baronets were required in return for the new honour to subscribe £1,095 to the King, being the estimated cost of maintaining thirty soldiers for three years.

On 22 May 1611 eleven baronets were created, of whose descendants only the Bacon and Shelley baronetcies survive. Since the first man honoured at the ceremony was the second Sir

Nicholas Bacon, he became the first baronet of Redgrave and premier baronet of England, a title accorded to all inheriting the baronetcy. Payment for the honour was soon abandoned but a baronetage of Ireland was created in 1619, which lasted until the Union with Ireland in 1801, and five years later the Nova Scotia baronetcies, the only baronetcy able to by held by a woman, continued to be created until the formal Union of England and Scotland in 1707.

The new baronet had seven sons. On his death in 1624 his eldest son succeeded him and when he died in 1649 without issue his brother, Robert, became the third baronet. Meanwhile Bacons seemed to attract baronetcies for in 1627 Sir Nicholas's third son, Butts, had become a baronet in a separate creation, that of Mildenhall in Suffolk, thus strengthening the family's original ties with Suffolk rather than with Norfolk.

Fame of a very different kind came to Sir Nicholas's seventh son, Nathaniel (1585–1627), who was the finest artist of his time and the first amateur painter of note in England. He studied in Italy but was also influenced by Flemish artists. Six of his works have survived. A fine self-portrait hangs at Raveningham and the earliest known British landscape in the form of a miniature is in the Ashmolean Museum at Oxford. The remaining paintings are at Gorhambury and include a still-life known as *The cookmaid with dead fowls*, described as 'the first real woman to appear in British art'.

One other seventeenth-century Bacon, although not in the direct line of descent, greatly interested Mindy. As a young man this Nathaniel Bacon (1647–76) had emigrated to Virginia, where he became a wealthy planter on the James river. Angered at the failure of the Governor, Sir William Berkeley, to give planters adequate protection against attacking Indians, or, of more importance, any share in the government of the colony, without waiting for a commission he led a force against the natives. After the successful ending of this raid the planters, with Bacon as their inspiration, began to demand sweeping changes in the government. The Governor panicked and fled to the eastern shore. Seizing his opportunity, Bacon captured and burned Jamestown and then proceeded to plan tax and franchise reforms in a newly elected House of Burgesses, action now known in American history as Bacon's Rebellion. Before he could achieve his aims he caught a fever and died.

In March 1976 Mindy, as Lord Lieutenant of Norfolk, visited Norfolk in Virginia to take part in the bi-centenary celebrations of the Declaration of Independence. In the course of his visit he was shown Nathaniel Bacon's house, still called Bacon's Castle and embellished with his crest, one of the earliest surviving houses in the United States. On his return home, in a letter of thanks to one of his hosts, Mindy wrote: 'I have always maintained that had Nathaniel Bacon lived it is probable that you might have received your independence a good many years earlier than you did, because he did not like – and who can blame him? – taking orders from people 3,000 miles away.'

While Nathaniel Bacon pursued his colourful career in Virginia a third baronetcy, that of Gillingham, came to the Bacon family in February 1661/2 but as it became extinct a quarter of a century later it is of little interest in the story of Mindy's ancestry. However, two events of importance occurred during the first half of the eighteenth century.

It was the marriage of the 4th Redgrave baronet, yet another Sir Edmund Bacon, which brought the main branch of the family to Raveningham in south-east Norfolk. Ever since about 1275 the family of Castell had lived in the village and when, as his second wife, Sir Edmund in April 1713 married Mary Castell, the direct descendants of the Lord Keeper, who, in Mindy's words 'had lived all over East Anglia for a great many years', ceased their wanderings and settled at Raveningham. They perpetuated the name of Castell by frequently adopting it as a second Christian name and Mindy himself was baptised Edmund Castell. On the brass in Raveningham Church the name of the village is spelled 'Ranningham', which is how the name is pronounced by those who live there. The name means 'the home of the young ravens', but whether this refers to the birds or to some long forgotten family who once lived there is unknown.

The second event of importance in the Bacon history was the union of the two baronetcies of Redgrave and Mildenhall. For a century and a half the two Bacon baronetcies had continued independently but in 1755 Richard, 8th baronet of Mildenhall, also succeeded to the Redgrave titles as the 7th baronet, thus uniting the honours of the two branches of the family.

The Castells had for long been lords of the manor at Raveningham but no trace remains of the house which they occupied. Raveningham Hall, Mindy's home, was erected for Sir Edmund Bacon, the 8th and 9th baronet, in about 1750 by an unknown architect, on a hitherto undeveloped site. The present Hall farm is still surrounded by a moat and it may have been here that the Castells lived. There is greater evidence that in the fourteenth century a small monastic college with a Master and eight secular

Raveningham Hall. An engraving of 1818 based on a drawing by
J. S. Cotman

canons stood here before the monks moved to Norwich. Mindy, while deeply attached to his home, cherished no illusions that it compared in architectural importance with the great Norfolk houses like Blickling, Houghton, Holkham or Felbrigg. This is clear from a letter which he wrote in 1970 to a man anxious to include Raveningham in a book on Norfolk country houses, 'I doubt very much whether this house is of any architectural importance. As you probably know it is late Georgian, which was greatly added to by my father and, to a certain extent, pulled down by me. I am afraid, therefore, it is a hotch potch.' Nevertheless, it is a very attractive redbrick building, facing a magnificent lawn,

and a house which for the greater part of its history has been a
home.

The 4,000 acres which in Mindy's time comprised the Raven-
ingham estate was not the only property owned by the Bacon
family. During the nineteenth century some 10,000 acres near
Gainsborough in Lincolnshire passed to them. The family of
Hickman can be traced back to the thirteenth century but by 1826
Frances Hickman, the last surviving member, died bequeathing
about 5,000 acres of the Thonock estate to her cousin, Henry
Bacon, directing him to assume the name and arms of Hickman.
To this he agreed. His successor, Sir Henry Hickman Bacon,
Mindy's grandfather, had in 1853 married a rich heiress, Elizabeth
Beckett, whose 5,000-acre estate at Somerby adjoined the
Thonock lands. The two properties were joined, the name of
Bacon restored but the name of Hickman retained by many as a
Christian name.

Meanwhile, the fields presented to the Lord Keeper by Queen
Elizabeth I had long been covered with houses and, as now part
of Chancery Lane, had become an immensely valuable property.
Nevertheless, none of these three properties might have been
inherited by Mindy: he maintained that he was very lucky to have
inherited anything at all. Nicholas, his great grandfather, born in
1786, was a gambler and spendthrift, who squandered his money
betting on fighting cocks. He survived on a weekly allowance of
£3 (quite a large sum then) from his elder brother, Sir Edmund,
són of the builder of Raveningham Hall. He had married in 1813
a beautiful girl, Alice Bowker of Kings Lynn, by whom he had
four children and who survived, a formidable old woman known
as Granny Gogs, until 1888. 'The whole of the fortunes of this
family were governed by the fact that old Sir Edmund outlived
his brother. If he had not, then there would have been no Raveningham, no Chancery Lane, no Thonock, in fact nothing and we
can thank our lucky stars that he died when he did. I strongly
suspect that he lies in the vault in the church, which, I am glad to
think, is now absolutely full up and can receive no more of my
family.' It was a close run thing; Nicholas died in 1863, his
bachelor brother a year later.

2

Thonock and Raveningham

Between 1862 and 1890 no Bacon lived at Raveningham and the Hall was let. Mindy's grandfather, Sir Henry Hickman Bacon, had continued to live at Thonock when he succeeded his uncle and he remained there until his death ten years later. His wife, Elizabeth Beckett, had borne him eight children, five boys and three girls. One boy and one girl had died at a comparatively young age of tuberculosis but the other four boys – familiarly known as Hick, Nick, Tom and Dick – all spent their early years in Lincolnshire. Of these, Hick and Nick, respectively Mindy's uncle and father, were the most important influence on him.

Sir Hickman Beckett Bacon had been born in 1855 and had inherited the title at the age of seventeen. After a brief period of service with the Grenadier Guards he returned to Thonock and settled down in the cheerless family house, a mid-Georgian building, which had been re-cased and stuccoed in the early nineteenth century. Gainsborough Old Hall, one of the finest Elizabethan manor houses in the country and the meeting place for the Pilgrim Fathers in the seventeenth century, had belonged to the Hickmans until 1826 when it passed to the Bacons; but its gradual deterioration made it too costly to preserve and it became unsuitable for habitation. In 1949 Mindy leased it for a shilling a year to the Friends of the Old Hall, who began to convert it into a museum with rooms furnished for receptions. Eventually in 1970 the Ministry of Works assumed responsibility for its preservation on acquiring it from Mindy for £1.

Thonock Hall cannot have been a comfortable house to inhabit. The drinking water was pure and came from a pump in the back yard but no other water was safe; hip baths were provided as there was only one hot tap on the upper floors, said to be connected directly through the wall to an outside tank fed by rainwater and that when the tap was turned on frogs were apt to emerge; there were no coal fires and coke was burned downstairs, the bedrooms being heated when in use by big wood fires; there was no electricity and no form of central heating. Structurally the inside plasterwork needed much attention: a visitor leaning against a wall to inspect a Breughel painting at close range dislodged about a square foot of plaster. Except to re-paint the downstairs cloakroom, no decoration had been done since 1870.

Here, surrounded by a large domestic and estate staff, Hickman lived alone. He remained a bachelor all his life, for a passing love affair with an Austrian countess come to nothing. The sole relic of his love is a very heavy gold signet ring, given to Hickman by the countess and now worn by Mindy's daughter-in-law. On the inside is inscribed in French 'Jest not at love'. Hickman was throughout his life a very distinguished-looking man, tall, with a fine head and sensitive hands. When in London he wore very old-fashioned formal suits, green with age, which yet did not detract from his aristocratic appearance.

As a landowner Hickman was invariably kind to those dependent on him. If an estate worker in one of his cottages was in difficulties over paying his rent he was relieved to be told 'wait until you can'. To what extent the large number who ate their midday meal in the servants' hall at Thonock shared his belief that a liberal dose of cod-liver oil after meals was a sovereign remedy against colds, or relished the large supplies of it provided for them, is less certain.

Nor was it only those immediately dependent on him who mattered. It may well have been this concern for others which explains his friendship with Sidney and Beatrice Webb, the early Fabians, a friendship which differing political opinions did not affect. He had a great sense of public duty and was one of the original members of Lincolnshire County Council and its chairman for ten years from 1914. Here his hatred of waste in any form must have been very evident when accounts were scrutinized. Like many very wealthy men he was opposed to any form of expenditure which could not be fully justified. In his case, and even more in his younger brother Nicholas, prudence became parsimony and sometimes meanness.

This family trait, which to a much lesser extent Mindy shared, was typical of a widely-held Victorian belief that to spend unnecessarily, especially on one's own comfort, was a reprehensible form of self-indulgence. It was certainly held by Hickman's acceptance both of the discomforts of Thonock and of the condition of his clothes. It was said that his ancient top hat should have been placed on his coffin at his funeral and buried with him. Sandwiches provided for him when away at a meeting, if not all consumed, re-appeared at dinner to be finished. Having discovered from paying for the funeral of a child on his estate how costly such ceremonies were, he ordered a coffin to be made for himself of the roughest wood, which for a long time stood in the entrance hall at Thonock, a receptacle for sticks and umbrellas. After a visit to a school in which the blind were taught basket work he was not content with one coffin and at once ordered a wicker coffin to be made for him, as being 'easier to get out of on the Day of Resurrection'. When the day came for the wooden coffin to be used it was found to be too warped for the purpose and an oak tree was quickly felled for a new coffin. Perhaps only Stanley Spencer in his Resurrection paintings would have fully approved of the wicker coffin.

All four brothers were enthusiastic motorists in the early days of motor cars. Hickman was not content to drive at speed up and down the long Thonock avenue or, accompanied by his chaffeur, to take corners in surrounding lanes on two wheels; but with his hat tied on with a piece of string he raced at 80 m.p.h. on the Brooklands track. He was also very clever with his hands and he invented and made a brass carburettor, a design much in advance of its time. His innate kindliness could be seen when driving back to Thonock from Gainsborough with his open car crowded with children, who had surrounded him in the town, begging a lift home up the hill. Although kind-hearted, he was a complete autocrat and refused to accept that new-fangled ideas like traffic rules applied to him. Having no self-starter in his car he found it much easier to leave the engine running when the car was parked. Once, on being reprimanded for this offence by a young constable, he ordered the man to get into the car, drove him to the police

station and handed him over to a superior officer for a severe
rebuke. The poor constable was firmly instructed as to his future
behaviour: 'You must never behave like that to Sir Hickman
Bacon.'

Uncle Hicky could be a disconcerting host to a young bride.
When Mindy brought Priscilla to Thonock for the first time she
was greeted with the warning: 'You have made a great mistake
in marrying into our family. We all die of T.B.' Not all hosts
remove their shoes and socks in order to warm their feet in front
of an inadequate coke fire. Nor do many people carry with them,
and place on the post office counter when buying stamps, a
spittoon. Mindy was determined to show Priscilla the collection
of bottles which his uncle kept in his bedroom. On the plea of
showing her one of the pictures in the room they found a large
table covered with bottles of every description. Hickman, realizing
what Mindy really wanted to show her, explained the forest of
glass by saying 'My mother said you should always give your
stomach a nightly surprise.'

While stories of Hickman's pleasant eccentricities are legion and
still vividly recalled on the Thonock estate, his claim to fame
and family gratitude lay in his shrewd business sense and in his
remarkable skill as a collector.

The Colville Estate Ltd was a private property investment
company, formed about 1870, in which two senior members of
the firm of Strutt and Parker, the estate agents, appear to have
taken the initiative. The original property owned by the company
was in the Notting Hill and Bayswater districts of London but in
due course freehold and leasehold houses and offices were acquired
in Brighton, Croydon and Weybridge. In 1915 when Hickman
became chairman, a position which he held for thirty years,
Colville Estate Ltd was registered as a private company; the estate
was valued at £236,000 with mortgages and loans at £234,000,
of which Hickman had accepted responsibility for £105,000. By
1920 the mortgages had been paid off, thanks in no small measure
to Hickman's interest-free loans to the company, which by then
had amounted to £220,000. This had enabled him to avoid
payment of income tax and super tax on this part of his fortune.
Further skilled management in 1929 ultimately benefited his
nephews and nieces by issuing them shares, which he had bought

from his own resources. This generosity was made possible after 1915 when he had inherited the substantial fortune of his aunt, Mary Beckett. How the Chancery Lane property became part of the Colville Estate belongs to the later story of Mindy's inherited business acumen.

Of far greater general interest is Hickman's love of collecting beautiful things. His two youngest brothers, Tom and Dick, shared his enjoyment of collecting, an enthusiasm which did not characterize either Mindy's father or Mindy himself. Hickman began by buying old china, little of it really valuable and some of it broken. He then turned to pictures, which became a life-long interest. He always bought what he liked and not what was fashionable at the time; fortunately he was blessed with an eye for what was first-rate. He seldom paid more than a few pounds for a picture and it was only once that he paid as much as £200 for a Turner. Today his collection of some 400 pictures, largely water-colours and drawings, is the finest in private hands in the country. Apart from his own purchases he inherited from the Beckett side of his family some magnificent Dutch and Flemish oil paintings, as well as works by Richard Wilson, three unusual Cotman oils and fine Constable sketches. In due course all of his pictures, together with the china and his collection of exquisite fabrics, passed to Mindy at Raveningham.

Hickman's readiness to show his pictures to a visitor or to lend them to a gallery for an exhibition turned a little on his assessment of how much the visitor knew about painting and as he grew older his reactions to such requests became highly unpredictable. In 1937 Margaret Pilkington visited Thonock on behalf of the Whitworth Art Gallery in Manchester, where she was organizing an exhibition of the works of J. R. Cozens and J. S. Cotman. She had learned about Hickman's collection from a member of the firm of Thomas Agnew and she wrote an entertaining account of her experience.

> After a long wait at the front door 'eventually a tall, frail old gentleman in light tweeds came into the hall, saw me and opened the door. He looked at me rather severely and said "You have come earlier than you said you would". He then said "I suppose you know that I don't like lending my

pictures?" I said that his letter had made that clear ... He then took me upstairs. He is a beautiful old man, very distinguished looking, with a white beard and a thin refined face – rather austere but full of life and character. His hands are also very sensitive looking ... We went up the big staircase hung with pictures and into a large disused bedroom. Every chair and table in that room and the bed itself was covered with packets of old letters tied into bundles with tape – I imagine they referred to past loans or purchases. Under every piece of furniture and round the room were piles of empty frames. He opened a huge wardrobe and inside it were piles of mounted drawings. There for an hour I had a very severe test of my patience and tact. He would bring out a drawing and push it back before I had seen it properly.

He eventually decided that he would show me some of the Cozens drawings (the wardrobe was full of all sorts of old masters, Turner, Girtin, Wilson etc. etc.). This he did and then said I mustn't have the big ones because it would be safer to have the smaller ones. I had a mind to the possibility of getting some Cotman drawings, so chose out three of the smaller Cozens – explaining in each case the reason for my choice. This seemed to melt him a little.' Protracted negotiations followed. 'He decided finally we might have some [Cotman's] provided that he could find the frames belonging to them. Then for a painfully long time he insisted on searching through the piles of frames, obviously a task too much for him but my offers of help were refused.'

In the end Miss Pilkington succeeded in convincing him of her expert knowledge and of her readiness to assure him that the pictures would be framed to his satisfaction. She came away with five Cotman water-colours and three by Cozens.

Before leaving she and her companion were given lunch. 'The old gentleman by now seemed to think me much less formidable and he talked on all kinds of subjects ... He asked me if I would like to share his melted cod liver oil – he had an enormous spoonful which he managed very dexterously to get over his beard – then dipped the spoon in his wine and sucked it again.'

Mindy's father, Nicholas Henry Bacon, Hickman's eldest brother, was born in 1857. When Hickman inherited Thonock in 1872 Nicholas, at the age of fifteen, inherited Raveningham but he did not live there until about 1890. He had enlisted in the 4th/7th Royal Dragoon Guards and during the Egyptian campaign of 1882 he saw active service at the battle of Tel-el-Kebir. He retired in the following year. When sixty years later he took an Armistice Day parade of troops stationed at Raveningham, he told the assembled body of men that he must be almost the last surviving officer to have gone into action wearing scarlet. Mindy had suggested that he should say this but warned his father that he would not be believed, although it was the truth.

Temperamentally Nicholas was very different from his son, who, in the ease with which he quickly got on with all and sundry, resembled his mother. Nicholas, by contrast, was a very reserved man, self-contained and not dependent on the company of others. He was only fully at ease with those who worked with him on county committees or with many of his estate staff, of whom he was fond and who respected him. Those working in the gardens were never certain whether the warning cough which signalled his approach was natural or a kindly method of avoiding coming across a man temporarily resting upon his fork – a habit which Mindy inherited or cultivated. It is possible that his seriousness of manner and his lack of any great sense of humour sprang from the fact that his father had died when his mother was only 45, with the result that from a comparatively early age he had a deep sense of responsibility for her and his family.

Nicholas, who had almost no interest in his family's history, yet had the family belief that public service was a duty though, unlike Mindy, he confined his activities to Norfolk where he was a Justice of the Peace and a member of the County Council and of the Board of Guardians. Partly prompted by this sense of obligation but more by his interest in architecture he planned the building of two parsonages, a village school, improvements to many cottages as well as designing new ones for his tenants, and he added a storey and two wings to Raveningham Hall. One of the parsonages at Raveningham, *Orchards*, became Mindy's home after marriage. Had he decided to study professionally he could

well have become an architect and, as one villager said, 'meaning
no disrespect, we always called him Bricks and Mortar'. The
houses which he designed were certainly more convenient to run
than was the Hall. At the same time he was a skilful carpenter:
his enjoyment of wielding a saw out of doors caused alarm to his
family by his habit of standing with one foot on the branch which
he was sawing off.

As churchwarden of the Raveningham parish church and
patron of the living he was a devout traditionalist, firmly basing
his beliefs and his choice of the services on the Book of Common
Prayer. He declined to read the lesson at mattins, probably from
shyness, but he was anxious to ensure that everything structural
in the church – the oak roof, the pews and especially the abundant
family memorials – was of the highest quality and was well
maintained. He took pains to find the best incumbent available
when a vacancy occurred, one of the most popular being Mr
Failes, who altered the times of services to fit in with the hours
of milking. His final choice, Mr Parker, always refused to accept
any hospitality or presents of game from the Hall and had been
heard to confess his fear of contact with the gilded world of
Mayfair, not a milieu in which Nicholas would have felt at home.

In the story of Mindy's life it is Nicholas's relation with his
own children and the general atmosphere of Raveningham that
are important. In June 1893 Nicholas married Constance Alice
Leslie-Melville, youngest daughter of Alexander Leslie-Melville,
himself the youngest son of the Earl of Leven and Melville, head
of one of the oldest Scottish families. She grew up at Branston
Hall in Lincolnshire and it is now impossible to say whether the
news that her father had arranged the marriage with Nicholas
Bacon came as a surprise. Arranged marriages were not uncom-
mon in Victorian days. To her were born four daughters, thereby
strengthening the belief that no boy was ever born in Raveningham Hall. In his anxiety for a male heir Nicholas moved his
wife to London before her next confinement. Although this might
be regarded as being somewhat late in the process to affect the
issue, on 18 March 1903 Edmund Castell Bacon was born. The
safe arrival of Mindy was celebrated with a party for the family,
friends and tenants at which Nicholas in proposing the health of
his son and heir referred to his four daughters, Margery, Joane,

Bridget and Constance, seated in the front row, as 'my four little disappointments'. With the family line secure the arrival of a fifth daughter, Katherine, was not a serious disappointment. The family was complete. The name 'Mindy' seems to have been his own invention. As a small boy when asked by well-meaning grown-ups what he was called he used always to reply 'Edmund-Mindy' and as Mindy he was thereafter always known by all the family, except by his father, who never referred to him as other than Edmund, an interesting pointer to the rather formal relationship between father and son.

Whereas Nicholas was a respected and, to many, an awe-inspiring figure, Constance was loved and very much the centre of family life. She had the gift of relating easily and readily with all whom she met. She seldom came home from a journey without knowing the life history of some fellow traveller to whom she had talked. She said that she much preferred to travel third class on the railway as she found the people more interesting and helpful than first-class passengers. She would enter the compartment, look around and choose whom she would talk to. She also found that she could knit more easily in the third class as there were usually others doing the same. It was this genuine preference for third-class travel, more than the fact that even when travelling with her husband she was expected to buy her ticket out of her house-keeping allowance, which explained to their friends, the Gascoignes, awaiting them on the station, why Nicholas and Constance emerged from different parts of the train. Easily amused and entirely unconcerned about what might be thought of her, she saw nothing wrong in having Mindy brought out from the middle of a meeting in London of the Lloyds Bank directors to answer her telephone call. Both he and his fellow directors assumed that he was needed for some urgent matter, perhaps connected with the British Sugar Corporation. 'You have left your toothpaste behind. Can you get some more or shall I send this on to you?', was the purpose of her call. Her enjoyment of people was mirrored in her initial response when answering the telephone herself, 'Yes darling, who is it?' This interest in and concern for people was more seriously seen in the help which she gave in starting a district nursing organization in Norfolk. Each week she saw the local nurse, which enabled her to know who was ill in the neighbourhood and might need help,. When the First World War began she ran the Norfolk branch of the Red Cross for the duration of the war and in 1919 her services were recognized by the award of the C.B.E.

Nicholas and Constance to a great extent lived separate lives; but in his undemonstrative way he relied on her and was very restless if she were ever ill. His care for her did not lead him to find out for himself by visiting her bedroom. Sally Dowson, a grandchild, recalls how at the age of twelve she was asked by him if she had seen 'Mrs B' that day and if she was out of bed. To most people he habitually referred to her as 'Mrs B' but addressed her himself as 'You', or merely whistled to attract her attention. His extreme parsimony must have irritated her greatly. An early bone of contention was the introduction of a telephone, which he opposed as an unnecessary expense and an encouragement of family gossip. 'Ladies like to talk about people; I like to talk about places.' It was eventually permitted but sited in a small pantry at an inconvenient distance from the morning room, where the family usually sat. When his married daughter, Joane Crewdson, and her family were occupying a flat in the Hall and Mindy and Priscilla and family in another, every quarter there was a roll-call and an inquisition on the telephone bill. Each had to admit for which calls they were responsible. Constance became so exasperated that she offered to pay the whole bill herself. During the Second World War petrol had to be strictly rationed but it was not necessary for Constance to be driven by the chauffeur only to the end of the drive and then have to catch a bus into Norwich. An ample supply of petrol coupons was kept locked in a safe of which only Nicholas knew the combination. Once in an emergency, when Nicholas was ill in bed, Constance was forced to bring him downstairs to open the safe.

However, it would be wrong to infer any lack of affection for his wife. Many of his letters to her have survived and despite their curiously cold and inhibited style it is possible to detect a genuine affection, which he was powerless to express. They wrote regularly to each other when away and especially as old age afflictions, like rheumatism and arthritis, increased. Nicholas's letters testify to his abiding interest in railway travel. Exact times of arrival at various stations are noted, with curt comments on unpunctuality.

Constance is informed of the cost of everything on his journeys. 'I reached Gleneagles 1 hour late. It is a most luxurious hotel, wickedly so I think, and I can't conceive how it can ever pay. I shd hate such a place to stay at. I had dinner (8/6) and caught the train at 8.30 p.m.' 'My bill at Edinburgh was reasonable – 12/6 for bed and bath, 6/- & 3/6 for meals.' Nevertheless, it was important not to be extravagant. 'I found that the 4lbs bottles of plums cost 7/-. The 2lbs bottles cost 4/9 each (9/6 the two) but they are larger plums; but the others are quite good enough.' 'You were rash telegraphing to engage the Harrogate rooms when I was doing all the correspondence. *You* might have had to pay Mrs Egerton or the other people.' 'It has been a beastly day – very dark, so I did accounts instead of going out. I worked out an inventory of my clothes and coats and made it exactly £300.' There was no chance of escaping his quick eye where money was concerned. 'A bill has come in for £7 odd from Penwell & Sons, Lincoln, for shrubs. Sidney knows nothing about it. The order is in my name. It looks as if Priscilla has taken my name in vain. I shall sent it to Edmund.'

Yet amid this obsession with trivial sums and punctual trains there is an anxiety for Constance's health and a sadness that she should be in pain and away from home. Minor illnesses among his children are also recorded with relief when a temperature drops or a cold – about which Victorians made a ludicrous fuss – did not become serious. His wife and family mattered greatly to him.

In any account of family life at Raveningham it is important to remember how different this was nearly a century ago. Nicholas had been born in the year of the Indian Mutiny and despite living to the age of ninety never lost the Victorian attitude of a father to his children. As often happens, he was more relaxed with his grandchildren than with his children. In the garden with his grandchildren he would chat about their lives and their hopes for the future. Indoors, he would pass them with a grunt. Although Constance, in marked contrast, was warm and out-going, she in no way pandered to any weakness in her children. Their lives were spartan. There was no electricity in the Hall, no central heating, only gas. They went to bed with a candle to light the way; on winter mornings they broke the ice which had formed on top of the bedroom jugs. They suffered badly from chilblains but when hoping for at least a little sympathy, they were told: 'Never talk about health, food, money or yourself.'

There was no question of girls going away to school: that only happened to boys. They had to be content with being educated at home by two governesses, one English and one Swiss, in a cold school room with three outside walls. It was rare for friends to be invited to stay nor did they stay away with their friends. Nicholas's second daughter, Joane, remembers how homesick she was on her first visit away from home at the age of seventeen. As a family they went to London every spring, to Scotland in the autumn, while their annual summer holiday was spent at Filey on the Yorkshire coast, where they were joined by Bacon and Barrington cousins. At home they were expected to make their own amusements and they unavoidably became involved in the life of the village, helping with local activities and reluctantly sent to collect for various charities, including one for mental defectives. They came to know well all the village characters: Johnny Cable, the parish clerk, famous for his dirge-like responses to the Litany; Gerty Mendham, the village organist; the Jewish Amos Moses and his Welsh wife with her two statuettes of Jellicoe and Beatty on the mantelpiece – Jellicoe placed upside down as she disliked him, while Beatty, her hero, stood upright; and Mindy's special friend, Harry Moss, who worked in the Hall garden for fifty years.

Although the pace of life at Raveningham was leisurely in a smoothly run house with plenty of domestic servants, a strict pattern reflecting Nicholas's ordered day, was observed. Family prayers, conducted by him and attended by the whole staff, preceded breakfast. Nicholas was an avid reader of newspapers, preferably retreating to his study well away from interruption where he read his paper from cover to cover. Once a grandchild substituted the previous day's issue and was highly amused to watch her grandfather read it over again. Because of his love of railway travel one of his hobbies was to work out long and complicated train journeys all over the British Isles with the aid of a Bradshaw. Lunch must have been something of an ordeal. Except for the years before Mindy went away to school Nicholas presided over an entirely female establishment – his wife, five daughters and two governesses. He came to the meal last, ate very sparingly, spoke little and left first with the rather surprising order 'Last man ring the bell'. As his daughter, Joane, wrote years later, 'He did not enter much into our lives.' He seldom entered the nursery except to say Good-night and while his children were dutifully respectful they were in awe of him.

The Sunday routine was unchanging. There was the morning service in the village church to which the children had to walk sedately, each armed with a sixpence for the collection – some remember it as a penny – previously taken from a small embossed metal tray on their father's desk. A buttonhole of violets when in season awaited Nicholas on the hall table alongside his top hat. Once the service was over the children were allowed to run home but back in the house sewing and card games were forbidden on the Sabbath, though knitting was permitted. Hymns were the only form of music. In the afternoon Nicholas took them for a walk and there is no doubt that he enjoyed their company although inhibited from showing any great warmth of feeling. It has been suggested that his natural reserve was not eased by his realization that the outgoing, warm personalities of his wife and son could never be his.

In many ways Christina McGregor, their much loved Nanny, was the greatest influence on the children in their earliest days, for much more of their time was spent in the nursery, as was then customary, than with their parents. Their memories of her remained throughout their lives. She adored Mindy with his ash-blond hair and rosy cheeks and she certainly spoiled him. Joane and and Katherine recall that 'we all played second string to him', but accepted this. To a lesser extent, as the son and heir, his parents also spoiled him but surprisingly he himself never seemed to be spoiled by it. Scottish, small and upright, high-principled and a strict Sabbatarian, Nanny put cleanliness at least on a par with godliness. 'How she scrubbed us – with square chunks of soap cut from a bar with a hot knife. She did not care overmuch if we were smart so long as we were clean!', wrote Katherine. In a corner of the nursery was 'a wooden stand holding a holland bag for dirty washing where, to our shame, Nanny put us if we were naughty'. Her favourite maxim, which she hoped would influence her charges, was hung on a hunting horn:

Do what you can, being what you are,
Shine like a glow worm if you cannot as a star.
Work like a pulley if you cannot as a crane,
Be a wheel greaser if you cannot drive a train.

But life with Nanny was enjoyable. It was she who took them to
Brundish wood to pick primroses; as they grew older there were
daily bicycle rides with her; she played halma and other games
with them in the evening; on Guy Fawkes night she was adept at
extracting roasted chestnuts from the bonfire; and in winter she
made 'ices' for them from jam and newly fallen snow.

To a modern child this circumscribed life would appear intol-
erable but it would be quite wrong to suggest that it was an
unhappy life. Looking back on it Mindy's sisters realize that the
predictable routine gave them a sense of security which was
invaluable. 'Rav' they remember not only as a beautiful but as a
happy and welcoming home. There were always new books from
the library lying about and there was plenty of time to enjoy
them. The staff seldom changed and when in later years the
married children came back on a visit they were welcomed by
familiar faces and heard the remembered sound of the clock over
the stables chiming the quarters, leading villagers in the days
before radio to enquire 'Have you heard Bacon go?' But for
Mindy this life ceased, at least in term time, when at the age of
eight he went away to school.

3

Growing Up 1911–22

Mindy loved Raveningham. He gained as much as his sisters from a secure and affectionate home life and he grew to share his father's love of landscape. Nicholas would sit happily for a long time quietly enjoying the Scottish mountains, the Lake District fells or the vast Norfolk skies. But Mindy was more fortunate than his sisters in being encouraged to have wider interests. While still quite small he enjoyed feeling that he was helping on the Hall farm and as soon as he was old enough he was taught to shoot, which he loved. Hearing that the village postman had died, his immediate reaction was to ask, 'who shot him?' His heart was early set on making the Army his career, a choice perhaps influenced by his father's brief experience of soldiering. For the moment he had to content himself with playing a then popular game called *L'attaque*, in which two armies of small upright pasteboard cards, plain on the side facing the 'enemy' but with various figures ranging from generals to privates facing the player, were launched at each other across a draughts board. Each side also had a sinister spy, inadequately concealed behind a tree, and some lethal 'bombs' to help.

At the age of eight Mindy escaped from governesses and went away to board at Wixenford, a preparatory school near Wokingham. The school no longer exists but in its heyday was very successful, with one of its headmasters, E. P. Arnold, being elected chairman of the Preparatory Schools Association in 1897. It flourished until the 1920s but dwindling numbers of pupils at the end of the decade forced it to close in 1934. Three years later its buildings again came to life when the well-known preparatory school, Ludgrove, took them over.

Among Mindy's contemporaries was Kenneth Clark, the art historian, who has written an entertaining, but not very flattering account of the school in his autobiography. He claimed that the three partners who ran the school were men of slender academic attainments and that the pupils were either sons of titled parents or of rich social climbers. Nearly every boy was destined for Eton. It was fortunate that the standards then demanded for entry to Eton were not as high as they have subsequently become, for, if Clark is correct, there was an almost total lack of scholarly teaching. That it was a school in which the boys were happy he had no doubt but for himself he regretted the lack of disciplined learning. However, in July 1916 Mindy left Wixenford, having been at least sufficiently well-grounded to pass into Eton, but without achieving any great distinction in the examination. Fifty years later Lord Clark, as he became, visited Raveningham to study a particular picture which Mindy owned. The two men had not met since leaving Wixenford but Mindy remembered the appropriately ridiculous schoolboy nickname bestowed on Clark and he used it to welcome him. Clark was not amused. So perhaps his account of their preparatory school was not wholly fair.

Mindy entered Cattley's House at Eton in September 1916, followed a 'half' later by his friend, Julian Gascoigne, a future distinguished Grenadier and Governor of Bermuda, with whom he 'messed'. Cattley was a kindly but not very exciting bachelor, who, in Mindy's and Gascoigne's opinion, harped excessively on the honour of the House. A boy caught smoking had not, like countless others, merely broken a school rule but was also morally guilty of letting down the House honour. He pursued the extraordinary hobby of collecting pictures and cartoons of people with strangely shaped noses. It was an exceedingly difficult time for any Tutor to run his House. Food was never sufficiently plentiful for healthy boys; most of the young masters had volunteered or been called-up – conscription had been introduced in January 1916 – and no Eton master or boy could ever forget the Head Master at Sunday evening chapel reading the names of those who had been killed in the previous week, often names of those who had been boys at Eton a few months earlier.

Mindy was never a great games player; in Eton parlance he was a 'wet-bob', that is he rowed in preference to playing cricket, which he later regretted. Nor was he ever academically distinguished. All of his reports have survived and certainly in his first two years there are clear suggestions that he did sufficient work to avoid trouble but no more. A generation later all his children earned the same comment in their school reports. Many masters commented on his handwriting, which George Lyttelton found 'mean and hideous'. Cattley's end of term letters to Mindy's father speak of his having 'been rather lifeless and listless as far as his work is concerned and inclined to be dreamy and generally not enough on the alert ... Please stir him up and rouse his ambition.' At the end of 1917 he complained that Mindy was 'careless about his books, leaving them about thoughtlessly and not knowing where they are'. But the letter continues, 'He looks rather fragile sometimes and, no doubt, his present lack of physical vigour reacts upon his working powers to some extent.' In April 1918 he wrote: 'As he gets stronger he will, I am sure, do better by his work.' Not surprisingly in July of that year Cattley admitted that as Mindy had succumbed to Spanish influenza, which was taking an alarming toll of lives throughout the world, this had had some effect upon his work! However by the end of the year, 'I do not think he is capable of working at high pressure for any length of time'.

Throughout his Tutor's letters there is scarcely a hint of what was really happening. Mindy in his years at Eton was growing at an unusually fast pace and, while his efforts were not commensurate with his abilities, it is clear that he had completely outgrown his strength. Although no medical evidence survives, it is possible to hazard a guess that he was emotionally a late developer.

However, Cattley, for the most part, thoroughly approved of Mindy as a person. His December 1918 letter ends, 'My good opinion of him remains unchanged. He is a wholesome and simple-minded boy and his happy nature is a blessing to others besides himself.' This good opinion lasted until April 1920 when Cattley had to complain about Mindy's 'ragging at tea ... food thrown about ... and crockery broken by unfair wear and tear ... He is just in that part of the House, that more than any other, gives a House its name and reputation, because boys then are in a betwixt and between stage and do not quite realize what they are unless they take the trouble to think.' A strange comment on a boy of seventeen. It is true that over sixty years ago boys were less mature at seventeen than they are today and it may be another pointer to Mindy as a late developer. Far more likely a cause of this not very serious fall from grace in his Tutor's eyes was a growing sense of frustration, which he and Gascoigne experienced. Mindy was by now certainly bored with 'the honour of the House' and he was far from being a 'simple-minded boy' but by July he was back in his Tutor's good books.

From his young days Mindy had set his heart on a career in the Army and he hoped to enlist in the 60th Rifles. It is interesting to note how markedly his work improved after being transferred to the Army class. 'Edmund has made an excellent start in Army class', Cattley informed his father in July 1918. 'The Sandhurst standard has been raised but there is no reason to doubt that Edmund will pass when his time comes.' For good measure Mindy won a Divinity Prize that 'half'. At a time when his behaviour had unduly distressed his Tutor his subject reports augered well 'for his success when he tries to pass into the R.M.C.' In July of the following year Cattley commented on his excellent health and spirits and that 'he is clearly ready to take all trouble to pass into Sandhurst'.

Then, probably during the summer holidays, the blow fell. According to the regulations in force at that time men were not encouraged to enlist unless they intended to make the Army their career. Mindy, with his life-long love of the Army, must certainly have intended to make soldiering his career or at least to serve in his regiment for an acceptable number of years. Nicholas now insisted that it was Mindy's duty, by reason of his inheritance, to manage the Raveningham estate in due course and to play his part in the life of the county. This being so, he forbade his son to continue to prepare for Sandhurst. Presumably it was impossible for Mindy to do other than obey his father: it was a bitter disappointment and it is impossible to exaggerate the effect which his father's decision had on him.

Mindy, in the normal course of events, had another year at Eton. Now with nothing to aim for a full year more seemed pointless. There was another reason why neither he nor Julian

Gascoigne wished to remain at school. When the war ended in November 1918 they were both half-way up the House in seniority. The terrible casualties on the Western Front had necessitated quick promotions to positions of authority within the House before, all too swiftly, being called-up. Once the call-up had mercifully ended boys were able to remain at Eton for much longer and this temporarily caused a blockage in the normal promotions. As a result Mindy and Gascoigne, along with their contemporaries, were victims of an inevitable check to their hopes of exercising authority in a House with too many senior boys. Much as they had enjoyed Eton it seemed useless to stay until July. They both left in December 1920 with a feeling of frustration, which added to Mindy's far more serious feeling of disappointment. He must have envied Gascoigne, who left for Sandhurst: he himself was accepted for entry to Trinity College, Cambridge in October 1921, in happy ignorance of the stiff academic hurdles which candidates for entry to that college would face after the Second World War.

In December 1920 Cattley wrote his final summary: 'We are all very sorry to lose Edmund ... I have always been very fond of him and there is something charming about him. He is simple and intelligent and straightforward and cheerful ... He has not had a distinguished career but he has done his best all round and in his quiet way he has done good to his fellows. He met his disappointment about the Army in exactly the right spirit, as I should have foretold he would. I wish that his Eton career had been longer. Anyhow he should have nothing to regret in it. I certainly have nothing. My only regret is that he has left.' Those who knew Mindy twenty years later will detect the emergence of certain easily recognizable characteristics in his Tutor's second and third sentences but as yet there was little sign of powers which must have been latent though undeveloped. His Tutor does not seem even to have suspected their existence.

If Mindy was leaving Eton in December Nicholas had no intention of allowing him to be idle in the nine months before going up to Trinity. In a letter of December 1920 to Constance he said that he had arranged for Mindy to go to a private coach, who tutored two or three boys near Nuneham Park in Oxfordshire. 'I settled for E. to go there on Jan 20. Doubtless he will have to remain till the end of the summer term – otherwise he will forget everything.' There was some talk of Julian Gascoigne joining Mindy there but nothing came of the suggestion as the man who looked after the boys 'was not an Army crammer and did not know much about the work'. It proved to be a pleasant house in which to live, with a tennis court and a boat house on the river two fields away but Mindy, who had already been accepted at Cambridge, must have slightly resented being sent to a crammer.

It was customary at Cambridge for most freshmen to spend their first year in lodgings and then to be given rooms in College for the remainder of their undergraduate life. Mindy shared lodgings at 9 Portugal Street with Humphrey Gibbs, an Eton contemporary but not a close friend at school, although their families knew each other well. Gibbs was to become a life-long friend, whose niece Mindy would one day marry. As both intended to farm, they began to study agriculture and estate management. Apart from the work it was a good life. Newmarket races were close at hand and Mindy was able to arrange shooting for them both. The carefree undergraduate existence which characterized the immediate post-war world both at Oxford and Cambridge was a pleasant contrast to the restrictions of school's rules and work with a crammer. 'Please ask Nanny to send me a white stiff evening shirt and collar. I think I had better have two for May week. I am only going to two dances.' On second thoughts he altered two to one and removed the 's' from 'dances'. 'I went up to London on Friday with Humphrey Gibbs and went to two plays, *Tons of Money*, which is simply priceless and *Sally*. We stayed in the Gibbs' house, which was nice and cheap.' It is clear that he had inherited something of his father's financial caution. He was able to go to Thonock occasionally and it would appear from a letter that his Uncle Hicky had presented him with a motor bicycle to ease his journeys from Cambridge.

However, the strictly academic approach to agriculture, which they obtained, bored both Mindy and Gibbs. 'Never saw a bloody cow', as the latter recalled. At the end of their first year they agreed that they had had enough and both decided to leave Cambridge. The College, as years later Gibbs expressed it, was 'uninterested'. In later life when they had both made a name for themselves in their different spheres, they were wryly amused at being welcomed back to the College as Trinity men of distinction.

Looking back on it Mindy always regretted the rather rash decision to leave Cambridge. He often said that he wished that he had completed a Tripos course and had chosen to read history or some allied arts subject rather than agriculture. With his departure from Trinity his formal education ended. He had enjoyed much of his time at Eton and his brief flirtation with Cambridge but in the end there was remarkably little to show for it all. One can only guess at his innermost thoughts as he now turned to seek a more practical approach to farming and estate management, frustrated at being unable to pursue the career on which he had for so long set his heart.

4

In Search of an Identity 1922–39

Once they had decided to leave Cambridge Mindy and Gibbs arranged to become pupils on the Duke of Newcastle's estate at Clumber in Nottinghamshire. Here, under the excellent guidance of Mr Elliott, the Duke's agent, they began to gain the practical experience which they had not found in Cambridge. They lived together in Sparken Cottage at Worksop, which Mindy told his mother was 'most comfortable. It is bigger than I expected and has got a big downstairs sitting room. The House Keeper is very nice and cooks well ... All my things arrived safely, including my motor bike ... We went to church here to-day, not much of a place as the service was long and the sermon rotten. We are trying somewhere else next time. There is only one other fellow here besides us.'

He and Gibbs lived very happily together. There was a 'good deal of tennis here every Saturday and old Elliott is quite good'. A long request for his fishing rods was sent to his mother telling her of the good trout fishing available. In the autumn and winter there was plenty of shooting and the two friends claimed that they had no need to pay any butcher's bills between November and March as they shot so much game. At weekends they often stayed in each other's homes or with Hickman at Thonock. They careered around the countryside on Mindy's motor cycle with Gibbs astride the pillion, an uncomfortable means of transport for two very tall men. Later Mindy replaced the motor cycle with a small Austin Seven, which was once picked up and turned round with both men in it. They had driven into a crowded garage and the garage hands thought this the quickest way of extricating them. It was on one of the weekends at Gibbs's home that he was introduced to his friend's very beautiful niece, Priscilla Ponsonby, then aged eighteen. Afterwards, Mindy casually commented, 'that girl will make somebody a first-class wife some day'.

It was while he was at Clumber that Mindy first hoped to join the Norfolk Royal Field Artillery then being formed to replace the Norfolk Yeomanry. Lord Bury, the commanding officer, so he wrote to his father, 'said that it was to be run on the *most economical lines* and as there is practically no chance of a Special Reserve for some considerable time I think perhaps I had better join it, as I do want to get into some branch of the Army ... You never offered any objection to my joining the 60th S.R. and now that it will not be started for years ... I think I might join the Gunners ... I do hope that you will let me join.' At the time of writing this letter Mindy was twenty but still felt that he should not join the regiment without his father's approval.

After two years at Clumber Mindy and Gibbs parted. As a younger son Gibbs had no prospect of inheriting the family lands and he decided to leave England and farm in what was then known as Southern Rhodesia. With insufficient capital he could not take the advice of Sir Charles Ponsonby, Priscilla's father, whose business interests in East Africa gave him a knowledge of where best Gibbs should settle. Eventually he bought land near Bulawayo, which he began to farm in 1928 but it was at first to prove an expensive investment owing to the need for constant irrigation and the consequent building of a dam. Although their ways diverged Mindy remained Gibbs's closest friend and in later years when Gibbs became Governor of Rhodesia Mindy was to prove a staunch ally during the grim days of Ian Smith's Unilateral Declaration of Independence.

Meanwhile in 1924, after completing his training at Clumber, Mindy was employed as agent on the Throckmorton estate at Coughton in Warwickshire. Coughton Court had been in the hands of the Throckmortons, one of the leading Roman Catholic families in England, ever since 1409. The mainly Elizabethan house was steeped in history: it was here that the wives of those implicated in the Gunpowder Plot awaited the result of the trial; as a Royalist stronghold in the Civil War, the house was seized by the Parliamentary forces and later bombarded by the Royalists;

it was further damaged during the reign of James II. This historic interest appealed to Mindy but to be agent was no easy assignment. He was not paid well and was not even provided with a bicycle on which to travel round the estate. As the family was expected to live off the estate it was up to him to ensure that it made a profit. This was because Lady Throckmorton had been widowed and there was very little available money. 'It was the best training I ever had', he used to say.

At the same time he very quickly became almost a member of the family. He was known to the children, with typical schoolroom humour, as 'Streaky'. Ann, one of the daughters, remembers having tea with him from time to time in his house, about a quarter of a mile from the Court, where he was looked after by a cook-housekeeper. Here he introduced Ann Throckmorton to all his favourite authors – John Buchan, Ian Hay and 'Sapper'. He was immensely popular with all the estate workers and with the whole village, where he started a troop of boy scouts and formed a football team. He bought himself a horse, occasionally hunting with the North Warwickshire, but he never really enjoyed hunting and much preferred beagling. Mindy's parents, as strict Protestants, had some doubts about their son and heir coming into a Catholic household but his mother was reassured when, on her first visit to Coughton, she was told that as her son was practically a member of the family, there could be no danger of his falling victim to the charms of any of the attractive Throckmorton daughters. In fact, religious differences never proved a difficulty. When the village idiot decided to become a Roman Catholic the Throckmortons enjoyed Mindy's nickname for the poor man – the Triumph of Rome.

Mindy remained at Coughton until 1927 when Sir Robert Throckmorton succeeded his grandfather as 11th baronet. His father, Courtenay, had been killed in action in 1916. Mindy's final task as agent was to organize the festivities which marked the new baronet's coming of age. Before returning to live at Raveningham he spent the greater part of a year abroad, studying farming practice in Australia and South Africa and grass management in New Zealand. On his way home he stayed in Rhodesia for about a month with Humphrey Gibbs. It was very cold when he arrived and he said how pleasant it would be to have a fire. Gibbs apologized and explained that his house had no chimneys. Mindy arrived home, well equipped with much practical experience behind him, to take over the 4,000 acres at Raveningham, aided by a professional estate agent and a farm manager.

That his father believed that Mindy had been a success at Coughton is clear from two letters written to his brother, Hickman. In October 1925 he had written: 'I think you would like to know that I have just transferred to Edmund 1572 acres of land, forming the outer ring of the estate, in order to save some death duty . . . There is a rent charge on it in favour of my widow. That constitutes a brake on folly but Edmund is very sound and he learned a lot from Elliott at Worksop. Of course the control, income and expenditure continue to be with me but separate accounts have to be kept.'

The whole estate was made over to Mindy in 1924 when he was twenty-one and a year later his father wrote to Hickman: 'I think it is a very good thing that I persuaded Edmund to give up cramming for the Army but to take up Estate Agency instead. He is very keen about it and he knows a lot for his age. His Superior Agent in London . . . said he had never had so little trouble with tenants on the estate. Edmund even made a small farm pay well.'

'He is very keen about it.' That in the years after the Second World War Mindy became the leading figure among East Anglian agriculturalists, deeply involved in policy at national level and greatly attached to his Raveningham and Thonock estates is beyond question. It is by no means so certain that in the decade between leaving Coughton and his marriage he found fulfilment in his enforced occupation. Few, if any, who knew him intimately during his twenties and early thirties have out-lived him and it is now only possible to guess at the effect of some years of uncertainty and lack of satisfying purpose, which, in the belief of one who had heard tell of these years, left him for a time secretly frustrated and unsure of himself. One of the puzzles about Mindy's career, on which several have commented, is the striking contrast between the years before and after the Second World War. Before 1939 there was very little hint of the outstanding personality which was to develop so swiftly after 1945. The years before the war are, however, important in the story of Mindy's psychological growth. Sufficient evidence exists to confirm a belief that the Mindy who was to bestride the East Anglian world like a colossus did not easily find a contented outlet for his immense nervous energy.

It is not difficult to imagine what Mindy's thoughts might have been on returning from his travels abroad. Eton had been enjoyable but his career there had been undistinguished; Cambridge, largely through his own fault, had been a failure; he badly needed to succeed. All who knew him and worked with him in his prime testify to his innate modesty but this quality need not have prevented him from having had an awareness of his own growing abilities and at the same time an uncertainty about how to be at full stretch in using them to the best advantage. It is interesting to speculate whether in these difficult years he ever came across Sir Francis Bacon's account of his own early life. 'Believing that I was born for the service of mankind and regarding the care of the Commonwealth as a kind of common property, which like air and water belongs to everybody, I set myself to consider in what way mankind might best be served and what service I myself was best fitted to perform.'

The management of the Raveningham estate, with all the help then available to him, cannot have been a full-time task. The game books for these years show that he could find time to shoot on three or more days each week. He was now twenty-five years old: with the best will in the world it is not easy for a man of his age, with great latent ability and an anxiety to serve his country and county to the full, to live contentedly at home, in the last resort subject to his parents. Nicholas Bacon, a Victorian by birth and outlook, especially in his relationship with his family, certainly approved of his son and knew that his own highly developed sense of duty had been inherited by him but in temperament and from his own upbringing he was unlikely ever to be close to Mindy. It was the sense of duty to the Bacon inheritance which had led him to oppose Mindy's wish to be a soldier. Mindy's disappointment over the Army had gone deep. Added to which was the fact, as in later years he told his wife, he never received any help and guidance from his father about the choice of an alternative career other than estate management. To Nicholas there was nothing further to discuss: his son's life would be a

1a. Hick, Nick and Dick, three of the Bacon brothers. Tom, the fourth brother, is not in the photograph

1b. Constance Bacon, Mindy's mother

1c. Nicholas Henry Bacon, Mindy's father

2a. Thonock Hall, Gainsborough

2b. Mindy's christening at Raveningham Hall, the family home, in July 1903

3a. Mindy with two of his sisters, Min and Biddy

3b. A festive occasion in early youth

3c. First term at Eton

4a. Mindy at the time when he was training on the Clumber estate

4b. Amateur theatricals at Tabley House. Mindy is fourth from the right; Priscilla on his left in housemaid's uniform. April 1936

5a. Mindy and Priscilla's wedding at Hunsdon Church. The Norfolk and Suffolk Yeomanry acted as guard of honour

5b. Mindy and Priscilla with Nicholas at his christening

6a. On a fishing holiday at Careysville on the Blackwater, County Cork, a property belonging to the Duke of Devonshire

6b. Mr Church, head gardener at Raveningham for 54 years. Joanna and Lavinia claiming the first strawberries of the season

6c. A Royal Forestry Society excursion to Raveningham

7a. With King George VI, Queen Elizabeth and Princess Margaret at the Norfolk Show in the early days of Mindy's Lord Lieutenancy

7b. Meeting the Queen and her family at Sandringham station before Christmas 1954

7c. With Queen Elizabeth the Queen Mother in 1963

8. Mindy and Princess Anne on an oil-rig inspection in 1969

continuation of his own. As a result a feeling of frustration, of pent up, almost explosive, energy as he sought the best method of release in service is not surprising. Yet only those very close to him were aware of his restless search for fulfilment and the self-assurance which only achievement could bring.

In the meantime if he could not join the Regular Army Mindy could do the next best thing and join the Yeomanry. In 1792 the Suffolk-born agriculturalist Arthur Young had suggested that the landowners and leading farmers in the county might place a horse at the service of the King, ready, if need be, to repel any possible invasion by Napoleon. His idea was enthusiastically adopted in many areas and the Loyal Suffolk Hussars, with Young as one of them, were raised in 1793 at Bury St Edmunds, thus becoming one of the oldest Yeomanry regiments in the country. The regiment remained in existence throughout the Napoleonic wars, despite the virtual removal of any serious threat of invasion after Trafalgar. Nor was it ever subsequently disbanded. The South African war gave the regiment its first chance of active service and when in 1908 the Territorial Army was formed the Loyal Suffolk Hussars became part of the new force. In the First World War the regiment fought with distinction at Gallipoli and in Palestine before ending the war serving on the Western Front. Peacetime brought a reconstruction of the whole Territorial Army and in 1922, with considerably less need for cavalry, the Suffolk Yeomanry united·with the Norfolk Yeomanry to form the 108th (Suffolk and Norfolk) Field Brigade, Royal Artillery.

It was in August 1923 that Mindy joined as a subaltern. The long history of the regiment appealed to his love of continuity. He was interested in the way that in order to meet the changing needs of passing years the Suffolk Yeomanry had been frequently transformed. From the original hussars they had become successively dragoons, infantry, horse gunners and, now, mechanized artillery. However, his belief in the virtue of tradition never prevented him from doing his utmost to ensure that any organization with which he was concerned met present needs and was not·ossified by excessive reverence for the past.

A man had to be a dedicated soldier in the 1920s to serve in the Territorial Army. The defeat of Germany had been achieved in 'the war to end war'. In 1919 Lloyd George had told the service chiefs that they had no need to plan for any major war during the coming ten years and this 'ten year rule' was repeated annually until 1932. Preparation for the unlikely outbreak of hostilities demanded a high sense of patriotic service. So on every drill night Mindy set out on the forty-five mile drive from Raveningham to Bury St Edmunds on roads which then fell far below modern standards and late in the evening the return journey had to be made. However, there were compensations. It was pleasant to serve in a body whose officers for the most part knew each other well from friendly contacts in the two counties; while men of all stations served in its ranks. Many of these were highly regarded by their commanding officers as valuable workers on farms, woodlands and neighbouring estates. Most Yeomanry regiments at that time were commanded by a leading figure in the county and when the two county branches were commanded by brothers-in-law of Mindy, who was himself to command the Suffolk Yeomanry from 1940, the Suffolk and Norfolk Field Regiment was often known as 'Bacon's Own'. Thus until the war clouds began to gather once agan after Hitler's advent to power in 1933 the profession of arms within the Territorial Army was a worthwhile and patriotic but not demanding occupation. For close relatives and friends to issue commands to one another has been likened, amusingly but unfairly, to a protracted negotiation.

One activity in which Mindy annually indulged in his early years was acting. It is difficult to account for the passion for amateur theatricals which took hold of so many of the upper and middle classes from the mid-nineteenth century onwards. Lord Melbourne, Queen Victoria's first prime minister, was an accomplished performer but it is doubtful if any amateur actor came near Charles Dickens and his friends in the intensity and professionalism of their work. However, some regular companies, like the Canterbury Old Stagers, who were founded in 1842, became famous for their annual productions during the Cricket Festival, meriting a review in *The Times*.

Many productions were the outcome of regular country house parties, such as those at Tabley House near Knutsford, home of the Leicester Warrens. Here in a theatre constructed in the stables and outhouses a play was performed each year soon after Easter. The cast was expected to arrive word-perfect and five days of intensive rehearsals followed, with only the afternoons comparatively free. The Tabley performances were unique in having Ian Beith – better known as Ian Hay – as producer. It was his custom to try out his latest play at Tabley before having it professionally staged in London. Mindy was a regular member of the company, acting in several plays both before and after his marriage. His most noteworthy performance was in April 1936 when he appeared as the clerical headmaster in Ian Hay's dramatization of his own novel *The Housemaster*. His performance was so good that Beith invited him to play the part in London. Much as he enjoyed acting it is highly unlikely that he seriously considered accepting the offer, later confessing that had he done so he would certainly have been cut off with the proverbial shilling by his father. However, his natural skill as an actor, with the actor's instinctive sense of timing, was to prove an invaluable asset in the innumerable speeches he would in later years have to make. Furthermore, a sense of occasion did not come amiss for a Lord Lieutenant.

If Mindy as a young man was uncertain of the right course in life to pursue, he had no shadow of a doubt that he wanted to marry Priscilla Ponsonby. If his sisters are correct, he does not seem to have been seriously interested in any other girl. According to her father's autobiography *Ponsonby Remembers* most Ponsonbys 'in early days were leaders, eccentrics, countrymen and sportsmen'. Colonel Sir Charles Ponsonby, who in 1956 became the first baronet, had been born in 1879. In 1912 he had married the Hon. Winifred Gibbs, daughter of the 1st Lord Hunsdon, by whom he had four daughters and a son – a family pattern which Priscilla would one day copy exactly. He served throughout the First World War with the 10th (Yeomanry) Battalion, The Buffs, in Gallipoli, Egypt, Palestine and France. In the 1920s and 30s, after qualifying as a solicitor, he became a director of several companies, mainly with interests in East and Central Africa. In 1938 he entered parliament as Conservative member for Sevenoaks, a constituency which he represented for fifteen years, and from 1940 to 1945 he was Parliamentary Private Secretary to Anthony Eden in the period when Eden was Secretary of State for War and then for Foreign Affairs. The family home was *Woodleys* near Woodstock.

Priscilla, the eldest child, was born in 1913 and came to know Mindy well through his friendship with the Gibbs family. She often stayed with her grandparents, Lord and Lady Hunsdon, during school holidays when her parents were in Africa on business. In her early years she lived in London until the age of twelve when, because she was delicate, her parents moved to Cobbe Place near Lewes, from which her father daily commuted to London after having taken some of his children riding before he caught the commuter's train. By 1930 Mindy, ten years her senior, was anxious to become engaged to her. He had come to Cobbe Place when camping in Sussex with the Yeomanry and they continued to meet at Gibbs family gatherings and occasionally at Raveningham. She was uncertain if she wanted to marry at once and claims that as she has always found it difficult to make up her mind she was naturally cautious about marriage. However, on 15 January 1936 Mindy won his bride and was married to her in St Dunstan's Church at Hunsdon in Hertfordshire. The reception was held at her grandparents' home, *Briggins* at Hunsdon. A wonderful partnership had begun.

In the year before his marriage Mindy, with a friend who lived nearby, had run a pack of beagles, which were kennelled at Raveningham. They both greatly enjoyed the sport and had plans for acquiring some basset hounds as well. This happened to be at a time when both men were to be married before long and they decided that hare-hunting and matrimony were both costly enterprises and that it would be wise to choose between them. Happily for Priscilla the wives won, the beagles were sold and the kennel man became Mindy's head gardener.

It is far from essential for husband and wife to be of similar temperament to ensure a happy marriage. Priscilla, lovely to look at, was, like many Ponsonbys, a girl of strong character, much more sensitive than might appear, unpredictable and because she was a quarter Irish in blood, with a disregard for time when absorbed in something which interested her. Mindy, on the other hand, was highly organized, punctilious about time and, at least outwardly, decisive. When Lord Lieutenant exact timing was important and several who devotedly served him in Raveningham Hall recall with amusement the sound of his bellow for 'Priscilla' as he waited impatiently for her at the foot of the staircase.

However different they may have been it is certain that the marriage vow 'in sickness and in health' was no light form of words. Priscilla's unfailing support of him not only made his Lord Lieutenancy outstanding but undoubtedly prolonged his life for many years after his serious heart attack.

They went for their honeymoon in a British banana boat to Jamaica and then in another banana boat, this time American, to Panama. In the British boat Christian names were only reached shortly before the end of the voyage: in the American boat they were Pip and Mindy to all the passengers within twenty-four hours. George V had died at the end of January and the Americans produced masses of their newpapers with banner headlines such as 'Will Our Wally Be Queen?' They were incredulous when told by Mindy and Priscilla that no one in England knew anything about Mrs Simpson. So, on discovering that this was a honeymoon trip the Americans gave them a special dinner with a menu containing Edward Soup and Wally Sauce.

On returning home they lived for a time in the Hall until *Orchards* was ready for them. This was not the easiest start to married life, not least because it was an inconveniently designed house for a large family. But Priscilla got on well with her in-laws and was never overawed by her father-in-law. To the surprise of the family she saw nothing wrong in writing a letter at Nicholas's sacred desk – something which none of his children would have dared to do.

In 1937 their first child, Joanna Constance was born; two years later a second daughter, Lavinia Winifred. The war clouds had been gathering ever since their marriage and it was clear that if war broke out Mindy, as a Territorial officer, would at once be called up. When war came on 3 September 1939 Mindy's feelings must have been mixed. He would certainly be parted from his family but he would be an active soldier at last.

5

Soldier 1939–82

In the summer of 1938 the 55th (Suffolk and Norfolk Yeomanry) Anti-Tank Regiment attended the annual camp, held, on this occasion, on the ranges of Okehampton on the edge of Dartmoor. It was the last time until long after the war that the yeomen of Norfolk and Suffolk were combined into a single regiment. Plans to form two anti-tank regiments from within the two counties were already far advanced. For in February 1939 the Chamberlain government decided that the rapidly deteriorating situation in Europe made an increase in the British armed forces inevitable. As part of this programme Hore-Belisha, Secretary of State for War, doubled the size of the Territorial Army, which resulted in dividing the existing combined Suffolk and Norfolk Yeomanry into two separate regiments. As a result of this re-organization the Loyal Suffolk Hussars emerged as the 55th (Suffolk Yeomanry) Anti-Tank Regiment, Royal Artillery and as such fought in the Second World War.

On 31 August news of the embodiment of the Territorial Army was announced over the radio. Mindy could not get to Bury St Edmunds quickly enough. As the news spread, from farms and estates, shops and offices young men left their work, hurried home to change into battle dress and say goodbye to wives and families before reporting for duty. Members of 217 and 219 Batteries were transported to Bury St Edmunds; 218 and 220 Batteries to Lowestoft. There was no shortage of volunteers to complete the complement of the greatly enlarged regiment but owing to the reluctance of successive governments to heed Churchill's warnings, equipment of all kinds was in woefully short supply.

Regimental legend tells how Sir Charles Rowley, Mindy's brother-in-law, who commanded the Suffolk Yeomanry, tossed up
with the commanding officer of the Norfolk Yeomanry for such
equipment as was available. It was sufficient for at most one
regiment only and Sir Charles lost the toss. In whatever way the
decision to allot the inadequate equipment was actually made, the
Norfolk Yeomanry from the start was on active service, sustaining
heavy casualties in defence of Calais and later fighting with equal
distinction in North Africa.

In April 1940 Mindy took over command of the regiment. For
a long while it was a frustrating task as the Suffolk Yeomanry
were destined to spend four years in Britain before D Day. During
these difficult years Mindy justified his position as commanding
officer in two ways. He himself became a recognized authority on
anti-tank warfare and was described as one of the few Territorial
battery commanders who could have taken charge of a Regular
battery without any difficulty. His other achievement was by
continuous effort to keep up the morale of the regiment as it was
denied the chance of active service and as it was moved from
pillar to post, endlessly training for battles in which many yeoman
doubted they would ever take part. From Suffolk the regiment
moved to Northumberland; then to Berkshire and on to Bedford-
shire; back once more to Suffolk before moving to Wiltshire.
Then followed a long move north, first to Yorkshire and thence
to Scotland for strenuous amphibious training at Rothesay and
Loch Fyne. Finally the regiment returned to East Anglia, being
stationed in Norfolk when news at last came that the D Day
assault was imminent.

It had been no mean feat to maintain morale and unflagging
keenness and by 1944 Mindy's men had become crack gunners.
He understood what the regiment was feeling for he fully shared
the general frustration. In January 1943 he had issued a New Year
Message to All Ranks: 'The fourth year of the war finds the
regiment still denied the opportunity of active service overseas
and I know that this comes as a great disappointment to us all ...
The monotony of three years of home service has been borne
with great cheerfulness by all ranks and in wishing you the best
of luck for 1943 I am confident that the tiring .days of waiting
will soon be over and that in the year of the 150th anniversary of

its formation the regiment will be given the chance once again of putting itself to the test of active operations.' He proved to be unduly optimistic but a year later in an address to the regiment he could give them succinct advice: 'When you meet the Boche you must KILL the Boche, or the Boche will KILL you.'

Not until the end of 1943 was it certain that the regiment, despite all its training, would take part in the Normandy fighting. Late that year Mindy with Priscilla was spending a night at Brown's Hotel in London where, owing to a porter's mistake, the luggage belonging to Major General Sir Evelyn ('Bubbles') Barker had been put in their room. In this way Mindy learned that his friend was also staying at the hotel. When they met he presumably gave the General an account of the regiment's frustrating years of waiting. The outcome of the meeting was that General Barker arranged for the Suffolk Yeomanry to be transferred from being part of the 79th Armoured Division to the 49th (West Riding) Division, which he commanded and under whom the regiment would play its part in the final offensive.

How did Mindy himself fare during this long period of home service? At times it was possible for Priscilla with Joanna and Lavinia to stay near where the regiment was stationed and thus to see something of him. But he must always have been wondering if once again he was destined to be baulked of openly proving his worth. He confessed to fearing that the war would be over before he had taken an active part in it. Despite its improbability, he occasionally imagined future jokes in the Norfolk Club about the only member who had served throughout the war without ever hearing a shot fired in anger. He may or may not have been aware that the more perceptive of his officers, wrongly believing that he had been sent down from Cambridge, suspected that he was anxious not to appear to have failed again. This large, genial and much loved and respected Commanding Officer had a very sensitive side to his nature, afraid of being thought to be, or found to be inadequate.

That he easily proved himself to be fully adequate to his task, a professionally competent soldier, always concerned for the welfare of his men, is beyond question. One who served in the ranks under him maintained that in the Army the two things which Mindy cared about for his men and which had to be of the highest standard were 'food and toilets. In other ways he were a bugger.' The man who said this believed that his C.O. had got his priorities right and was both feared and yet respected by those with whom he had found fault. Mindy's inner anxieties were only occasionally evident when he was faced with relatively unimportant and unexpected trouble. In the summer of 1941 the regiment had just completed a big exercise in the neighbourhood of Temple Guiting in Gloucestershire and it appeared that a rifle had been lost. This was not a trivial matter but instead of accepting that there were bound to be careless fools in any unit, Mindy's anger and alarm were out of all proportion. Preparation for an inspection by a higher authority was apt to cause him to panic. 'Windy Mindy' – a rather obvious rhyme – was a grossly unfair nickname coined on one of these occasions, though never containing a breath of criticism of his personal courage. It was admittedly a difficult command: it was no easy matter to keep control of four batteries, often widely separated, and inevitably from time to time things went wrong.

Once when Major Toms's battery was stationed near Reading he was warned to expect a visit from the Commander Royal Artillery accompanied by Mindy. He had been told that training was to proceed as normal. This he took at its face value. The guard was not specially selected and was certainly not the best available. The cook house and the dustbins were clean and the cooks had clean clothing. One troop was on leave; another was playing football. A miniature range had been fixed up in the vegetable garden with a model tank operated by a string and a .22 rifle fixed to a two-pounder gun. When this came to be inspected no one was using the range and the visiting commander believed that it had not been used. He was unimpressed when a subaltern ingeniously pointed out bullet holes in the wall behind the target. Mindy paled as Toms explained that it was recreation day and that training was proceeding along normal lines as instructed. Nevertheless, for the most part and whenever he himself was in personal charge all went superbly well and without a hitch. Preliminary stage fright ensured a perfect performance.

At last in May 1944 the order came to be prepared for D Day. Guns and tractors had to be carefully waterproofed for safe landing on the Normandy beaches and much had to be in a final stage of readiness. The work was to be completed if necessary in six days, though it was understood that D Day was probably still some weeks ahead. Thanks to Mindy's drive and energy the regiment was always well prepared but the approach of the moment for which he longed and his passion for exact timing increased his nervous energy and his anxiety that the Loyal Suffolk Hussars should acquit themselves efficiently as well as honourably. His Adjutant, George Lockett, who had heard the news of the approach of D Day before Mindy, had a more phlegmatic attitude to war than his admired friend and Commanding Officer. One of his hobbies was tapestry and he saw no reason not to continue this. Mindy came across him as he worked on a canvas and exploded in angry amazement.'You sit there with your bloody knitting at such a time', he shouted. This was not the moment for such employment. However, his admirably trained and eager yeomen were fully prepared when D Day came: in the words of Mindy's Second-in-Command, Major Brian Gooch, they were 'a perfect, and what is more, a happy fighting team'.

On 12 June 1944 the advance party under Major Brian Gooch, together with Major Toms and others arrived at the beach, anchoring off shore until the tide was right next morning. At the agreed rendezvous they awaited the arrival of Mindy and the bulk of the regiment. He with 219 Battery and other personnel crossed in a liberty boat skippered by a Scotsman. They were extremely lucky to reach Normandy. During the night the ship was hit by a large bomb, which went through the deck and buried itself in the coal bunker without exploding. The bomb put the steering gear out of order, making it almost impossible for the captain to guide his damaged vessel through the mass of shipping and to keep in line with the convoy. Inevitably Mindy and his men could neither land at the right place nor at the right time. In due course a naval corvette came alongside and its officer demanded in basic naval language what the captain thought he was doing. Quite unperturbed he replied that his steering had been broken and that an unexploded bomb in the coal bunker might explode at any moment. A sapper had informed him that if the bomb did not explode within twenty minutes the ship was probably safe. 'Deuced uncomfortable' was the sympathetic response to this information and the corvette sailed away. Lockett now had the embarrassing task of reporting their plight to the naval command and an American lighter was sent to their rescue. Mindy's impatience was by this time nearing exhaustion and was not eased by the strain of expecting an imminent explosion nor by the American insistence that nothing could be done until they had eaten their lunch. After half an hour they were ready. 'You've been a hell of a long time eating your lunch', shouted Mindy. 'We've had a hell of a lot to eat', came the laconic reply.

The regiment was soon safely on shore and after a few days, while the division assembled, it moved into line with regimental headquarters at Cabville. On 25 June 218 and 219 Batteries took part in the successful attack on Fontenoy le Pensil and at the end of the month 217 was busily involved in checking the German counter-attack. By mid-July the Regiment joined I Corps in the Caen sector. Regimental headquarters were now at Longueval; 217 Battery at Demouville, 219 at Cagny, 220 at Caverville and 218 in reserve. In these early days the regiment as a whole received an unpleasant share of German shelling by day and at night German bombers, guided by green perimeter lights, dropped their infernal cracker bombs. Even so cheerful yeomen complained that the danger was a nothing compared to the vicious mosquitoes which thrived on the damp clay soil.

Mindy must have regretted that in no sense did he exercise an independent command. His four batteries were under the orders of the infantry regiments to which they were attached, being largely used to protect the flanks of the infantry in defence. However, accompanied by Gooch, he was tireless in keeping in close touch with each battery. Owing to their exposed positions the guns could only be reached under cover of darkness; so the two men indulged in what they called 'early morning flights'. Once full daylight came it was wiser to remain under ground. At a little later date Major Toms recalls one of these visits by Mindy to his battery headquarters. 'He said he would like to visit our forward positions. We got into my Bren Carrier and drove up to the gun positions, which were well forward to prevent an attack by enemy troops. There was quite a lot of mortar shelling on the way as the German Observation Post could obviously see us. Neither of us said anything and we had a few words with each gun crew. On the way back I said the journey was a bit hairy and

Mindy agreed and was obviously doubtful whether it was the sensible thing to do. We both laughed about it afterwards; he thought I would suggest that we turned back and I thought he would order me to do so.'

Once Caen fell the great advance to the Seine began. It was a time of constant moves onwards through Chichibeauville, Bereauville la Campagne, Conoon (where there were no mosquitoes), Le Pin, Lac Noc Poulain and Valletot to the Forêt de Bretagne in the beautiful Seine valley. Here thousands of horses, wounded or bewildered by the bombing, had been abandoned by the retreating Wehrmacht. The Divisional Commander gave the yeomanry the task of dealing with them. It was decided that the easiest way of disposing of the carcasses was to push them into the river. Only later was it discovered that a unit about two miles downstream was equally busy pulling the bodies out, as the river water at certain tides was used for domestic purposes.

Once the Normandy break-out began infantry regiments no longer needed the anti-tank regiments to protect their flanks: 21st Army Group was attacking all the time. In a sense the Suffolk Yeomanry had successfully completed the work for which they had been so well trained. During the crossing of the Seine 220 Battery was responsible for traffic control on the bridge at Rouen and in the subsequent attack on Le Havre the regiment undertook a similar task for no anti-tank action was needed. The same was largely true in the final stages of the war.

After the action at La Havre it was officially announced on 6 October 1944 that 'on completion of tenure of command' Lieut. Colonel Bacon had handed over command of the Regiment to Lieut. Colonel Gooch. In fact Gooch's diary makes it clear that on 31 August Mindy had privately told him 'that he had asked to be relieved of his command and that Divisional Command and C.R.A. have agreed to my succeeding him'. As one who served under him later wrote, 'We were all shocked, surprised and saddened but took it as one of those things.' It is impossible to say with any certainty what prompted this move. He had been in command for over four years, longer than the average tenure; the specific work of an anti-tank regiment was largely over; he was now well into his 42nd year and the strain of the years of waiting in England and the responsibility of command in action must have taken some toll. There is a good deal of evidence that he continued to become unduly worried if everything did not go exactly to plan and a very sensitive man found the realities of warfare with the loss of comrades and the sight of the horribly wounded deeply upsetting. By the end of September 1944 he may well have thought it right to hand over command to Gooch, who had served him loyally for four years, and who he knew was longing to succeed him.

Mindy returned from Normandy to take command of the 22 Royal Artillery Training Regiment which was then garrisoned at Shoeburyness. As an experienced trainer of gunners he quickly won the respect and affection of his new command. 'We were all put at ease from the moment you arrived', wrote a fellow officer at the end of the war. A fitting tribute to Mindy's achievements is contained in a letter of August 1945 from the Commander Royal Artillery:

> I am sorry that I never had the opportunity of seeing your party in action except in displaying enthusiastic energy at Whitsun, but I know that Shoebury will be very sorry to lose you ... I will always remember your cheerful welcome in the dark days of 1940 in the Northern half of the X Corps Area, and I know how well your 'Loyal Yeomen' from Suffolk have performed through the hard periods of waiting to go to war (the fact that they eventually arrived was, I know, eighty per cent due to you personally) and on their record in the fighting on their eventual arrival ... It had been a genuine privilege as a Regular to have served as I have with so many first-class Territorial units in this contest. I am quite certain that the future of our Regiment is secure so long as senior Gunnery officers realise how much we owe to the Territorial Army.

On 22 March 1945 Mindy's services were recognized by a Mention in Despatches. Two days later the *London Gazette* recorded his appointment as an Officer of 'the Most Excellent Order of the British Empire in recognition of gallant and distinguished services in North West Europe'. In only one thing was he disappointed. He occasionally admitted to his family that he had felt a little sore that one of the D.S.O.s which were awarded to commanding officers at the end of the war did not come his way. He did not grudge Gooch his medal, but Gooch's tenure of command had been very short, and he felt that with over four years in command, including the hardest part of the Normandy fighting, he was equally deserving. It is known that many of Mindy's officers were angry and upset at his failure to gain proper recognition of his achievements and an attempt was made, but without success, to put this right.

Once the war was over and Mindy back at Raveningham he never ceased to take the keenest interest in the Yeomanry and its members. Inevitably peace brought change in the organization of the Territorial Army and a renewed need to maintain the morale of its members, reminiscent of the years after the First World War when he first joined. In 1949 the Suffolk Yeomanry once again amalgamated with one of the Norfolk Territorial regiments and ten years later, when the Norfolk Yeomanry converted to field artillery from light ack-ack, Mindy became Joint Honorary Colonel of the newly named 308 (Suffolk and Norfolk Yeomanry) Field Regiment R.A. (T.A.). This position he held until 1967, when a further reorganization of the Territorial Army eventually reduced the Yeomanry to being a Battery in a Yeomanry Regiment R.A.(V) with its regimental headquarters at Grove Park, London S.E.12! Whether Honorary Colonel or not, Mindy to the end of his life maintained his connection with his old regiment.

The appointment of Joint Honorary Colonel is occasioned when the Honorary Colonel is a member of a royal family and it is felt necessary to appoint a deputy more readily available to assist a regiment when required. For over half a century there had been a close connection between the Norwegian royal family and the Norfolk Yeomanry as King Haakon VII, who had married his cousin, Princess Maud daughter of Edward VII, had been Honorary Colonel of the Regiment. When in 1957 King Olav V, who had been born at Sandringham, succeeded his father, he also succeeded him as Honorary Colonel.

In November 1961 King Olav paid his first visit to the regiment, dining with past and present officers at Bury St Edmunds and reviewing the regiment next day on Angel Hill. He spent the intervening night at Raveningham, as he did five years later. On the second occasion he stayed two nights with Mindy and Priscilla, shooting pheasants in pouring rain after again reviewing the regiment. He proved a charming guest, highly appreciative of Mindy and Priscilla's warm hospitality. The sole difficulty for his hosts and their other guests was his habit of remaining standing in the drawing-room after dinner, unwittingly making it difficult for anybody else to sit down and relax. In turn guests would engage him in conversation while others took the chance of briefly sitting down in the adjoining room. On Sunday the King walked across the lawn to church. Alan Glendining had chosen the hymn 'Glorious things of thee are spoken' but had forgotten to tell the organist which tune to play. He thought it was going to be 'Abbots Leigh' and was horrified when 'Austria' was played, long familiar as the Austro-German national anthem. Glendining's profuse apologies after an otherwise excellent service were forgiven when King Olav said that it had been his grandfather's favourite tune.

There were two annual occasions when Mindy was with the Yeomanry which gave him untold pleasure and which he strove never to miss. Every April the Suffolk and Norfolk and Artillery Dinner Club met at the Cavalry Club in London with Mindy in the chair. When all were in their places he opened the proceedings with 'Gentlemen, pray silence for Pete'. This was the signal for the Revd Peter Partlett, the Suffolk Yeomanry's chaplain before and during the war, to say grace. Throughout the evening Mindy was the life and soul of the party. He knew personally nearly all who were present, talking to them all and making a point of welcoming any junior officer, as yet unknown to him, who might be present for the first time. When the evening ended he would, if possible, return to his hotel by bus; to take a taxi if alternative means of transport existed was an unnecessary expense – a view not always shared by friends travelling in the same direction.

This annual dinner meant a great deal to him. 'What I really resent', he wrote about one senior yeoman, 'is people like him pontificating on what ought to happen [about the Dinner arrangements] when he has never bothered to put in an appearance for ages; and I expect one or two more have done the same.' He saw no reason to change the form of what had for long been a happy and nostalgic occasion. 'I expect', he wrote in June 1980, 'there may be a demand for a "Ladies Night". I deplore this. There are

some things that are male preserves only, even in these days, and
I think a Regimental Dinner is one of them. However, there
again, if the majority wants to turn this into a sort of Gala by
all means let them do so. The only thing is that some of us
may feel that possibly this is not what we are looking for and we
may very well drop out. However, this is only a personal opinion.'

Mindy with his deep love of continuity regretted that this
feeling was not always shared by younger generations. This is
clear in a letter of October 1979 referring to the lack of care in
preserving the regimental silver. 'I am afraid the trouble is that
the modern T.A. Officer is not very interested in relics of the past
in the same way we are. At any rate I shall hunt out [the man
responsible] when I see him at the Cocktail Party and tell him
that he ought to pay more attention to the Old Guard, who really
belonged to the two ancient Yeomanry Regiments; because not
one of them served like we did with the old Suffolk or Norfolk
Yeomanry Regiment, who provided most of the silver. We
regarded ourselves as yeomen armed with guns; they regarded
themselves as gunners full stop! Therein lies the difference.'

It was not only the more formal occasions which Mindy
attended; he equally enjoyed dining with a small group of Yeomanry officers. On one such occasion it was decided that the main
course should consist of pheasant. No questions were asked when
a man who knew his way about the countryside offered to provide
the birds. As Mindy arrived for the dinner the man, who was on
guard at the gate, presented arms and then saluted. After the
dinner Mindy thanked all concerned for the evening. When he
came to the man who had been at the gate, he said how particularly
he had enjoyed the pheasant. Then with a twinkle in his eye he
added, 'But you should not salute an officer with a 12 bore rifle.'

Mindy's concern for the well-being and efficiency of the regiment extended far beyond convivial evenings. At the annual camp
held at various artillery ranges and twice at civil defence camps
the regiment underwent a spell of practical training. He invariably
joined his regiment in camp for two nights, no matter how far
he had to travel and, at times, regardless of his health. He watched
every section of the regiment deployed at its various tasks whatever the weather and he met old and new friends when they
returned to base. The sergeants' mess serenaded him before he

dined with the officers. Despite the passing years he never seemed
at a loss for a face or a name.

Colonel John Wilson tells of two of many such visits to the
annual camp.

> I recall his coming to Millom in Cumberland in, I think,
> 1963 for a Civil Defence Camp, disliked by all but one of
> those things that had to be endured. He ought not to have
> come at all as he was far from well. But come he did, all the
> way from Raveningham via London and a sleeper between
> Euston and Barrow on consecutive nights. He still did his
> thorough visit to the whole Regiment and it cannot have
> done him any good. On another, and better, occasion he
> came to Sennybridge ranges in Brecon and I recall meeting
> him at Newport off the South Wales Pullman. That was the
> time when a gun layer was discovered to have laid his gun
> in foggy conditions on the backside of a grazing sheep! This,
> apochryphally, had always been regarded as a very old
> chestnut of the Gunnery Staff but it really happened.

As he was driven around the camp area he plied Colonel Wilson
with ceaseless questions, remaining, even as he grew older, an
acute observer of people and seldom wrong in his assessment of
their capabilities. Soldiering was certainly in his blood and was
an important part of his life. However, in the light of all that he
achieved in the post-war years the county, and often his country,
would have been the poorer had his father allowed him to join
the Regular Army.

6

Farmer and Landowner 1945–82

On 25 September 1945 Mindy was released from the army. In the same year his uncle, Hickman, had died: despite his fears that tuberculosis would shorten his life, as it had of an elder sister and younger brother, he was in his 90th year. The baronetcy passed to his eldest surviving brother, Nicholas, Mindy's father. Only two years younger than Hickman he was unlikely to hold the title for long and in 1947 he died, also in his 90th year. To the end he had remained remarkably young in appearance. At his funeral service the Vicar of Raveningham, Mr Parker, overcame his fears of the allegedly gilded life at the Hall and paid a deserved tribute to Nicholas's 'rugged honesty and straightforwardness' and to his high sense of stewardship in the ownership of land. 'To him it was a calling, a vocation, a profession, a life work, demanding all his energies of mind and body.' In addition he contributed an obituary notice to *The Times*, which praised his virtues.

So on New Year's Day 1947 Mindy became the 13th Baronet of Redgrave and 14th Baronet of Mildenhall, Premier Baronet of England. Nicholas had inherited Raveningham when he was twenty-one and he believed it right that Mindy at the same age should take control of the entire estate. The Thonock lands had already passed to Mindy on Hickman's death, together with his collection of water-colours and drawings and the Beckett collection of oil paintings. It was a magnificent inheritance but one which he firmly believed should be held in trust by him for future generations. Thonock Hall, on the other hand, was a less valuable part of the inheritance. Although solidly built, to make it comfortably inhabitable was very costly. Before electricity could be installed cables would have to be laid from the main road beside the long drive to the house. Once made habitable it was a much bigger house than Mindy needed for his visits to Thonock and he leased it to a storage firm. Then, despite protests from some in the area, he decided to demolish the house in 1960. Meantime, Priscilla had found a small house, Ash Villa, in Gainsborough which was far more suitable. The Thonock butler who came to Ash Villa had never before turned on an electric light switch and after years of living in semi-darkness believed that no electricity was supplied until every switch was turned on.

At the time of Nicholas's death Mindy and Priscilla, with their first three daughters, were living at *Orchards*, the house originally designed by Nicholas as the Raveningham parsonage, commandeered for officers during the war and only recently handed back. The house was used by the anti-aircraft headquarters' staff, who looked after it extremely well. When on leave, Mindy with Priscilla used to come back to see the house and were delighted on one occasion to find the Colonel busy pruning the roses and others prodding the lawn to eliminate moss. They assumed that in due course Constance would leave the Hall and move into *Orchards*, while Mindy and his family took over the Hall as Nicholas had planned. Constance had other ideas. 'When one's reign is over it is time to move on.' She quickly moved out of the Hall but, never really a country lover, had no intention of remaining in Norfolk. She decided to live in London, so as to be easily visited by children and grandchildren; and in a very large flat in Ashley Gardens she continued to be the sheet anchor of the family, recipient and retailer of all the family doings. Here she began a new life, looked after by two ageing but devoted servants, happily entertaining on a scale which, perhaps with pardonable exaggeration, she claimed entailed giving a meal to about a hundred visitors each month, regardless of those who dropped in for a casual drink.

Her church in Westminster was St Stephen's, Rochester Row and here the Vicar, the Revd Anthony Tremlett, later Bishop of Dover, became a close friend. In days when clergy were more plentiful Tremlett had five curates and he used to make sure that they visited her and, as she grew older, brought her Communion. She like to tell each new curate that as a girl she had been confirmed by the saintly Bishop King of Lincoln, perhaps half-hoping that they might wonder if something of his saintliness had been passed on to her. As she grew more frail Tremlett became aware that something was troubling her. Eventually one of her daughters gave him the hint that as she had always laboured for good causes she was worrying whether she ought, despite increasing tiredness, to struggle to remain alive. Tremlett told her that with all old people, many of whose closest relatives and friends had inevitably died, the 'tug from the other side' was much stronger than the claims of this world and that there was nothing wrong in being ready to die. This gave her great comfort and, after giving her his blessing, Tremlett left her. Soon afterwards she died in peace.

Raveningham Hall today. A drawing by Louis Mackay

After moving into the Hall Mindy decided that he wanted to demolish the two wings of the house which his father had enlarged and make other smaller changes. The wings unnecessarily increased its size and their removal would restore it to something nearer its original and more attractive design. Unfortunately it was a bad time to carry out the quite considerable amount of work involved. In the immediate post-war years labour and materials were in such short supply that a licence had to be obtained for almost any work and would only be granted if the work were absolutely essential. His architect, Claud Phillimore, a personal friend, believed that the cost involved was sufficiently small that a licence was not needed. In the midst of the demolition another client of the same architect faced serious trouble for unlicenced large-scale alterations to his family home. Mindy was away when this news came and Priscilla at once ordered the work to stop until careful checks on the expenditure involved were made. To their relief they discovered that the planned changes lay within limits permitted by the government and the work was completed.

Ten years earlier Mindy had been a man uncertain where his true path lay, often unhappy and frustrated. Marriage, the war years and now big responsibilities at Raveningham and Thonock, the Lord Lieutenancy of Norfolk from 1949 and innumerable claims on his time account for a profound change as he grew into a man who dominated his county and who in the field of agriculture became a nationally respected figure. Mr Timothy Colman, a generation younger and his successor as Lord Lieutenant, watched this growth with admiration. With every new responsibility and every new opportunity for service, Mindy, he recalled, grew in stature. In the fostering of his own inheritance and in the countless tasks which he voluntarily undertook his natural powers of leadership flourished as he found fulfilment. Only one mark of early difficulties was never overcome – his habit of talking aloud to himself. People marvelled at his sense of authority and his outward appearance of being untroubled by all the problems which he had to face and the decisions which he was called to make. They never realized that Mindy was, as his family knew, a 'bottled-up' personality, who released his unseen tensions and sensitivity by pouring out to himself his anxieties and his unrestrained comments on those with whom he was dealing. This habit had its amusing side. The one-sided conversation often took place while he was having his bath and his daughters remember listening at the keyhole while he debated aloud the most suitable form of punishment for their latest misdemeanours. They at least were forewarned of what lay in store and might be able to take avoiding action. Nicholas, his son, recalls wanting a word with his father in his study and not venturing to enter on hearing the vociferous tirade directed against someone who had annoyed him. Only later did he discover that his father had been quite alone. With Beulah, his enormous dapple grey English mastiff, sitting beside him in the car, he had a sympathetic listener to his thoughts and one unable to disagree.

In appearance, dress and manner, Mindy could pass for a typical country squire. A giant of a man, 6 foot 3 inches in height and broad in proportion, with hunched shoulders, ash-fair hair, sharp blue eyes and blunt features, he was essentially a countryman. Dress, except for his uniform, mattered little to him and he was happiest when he could wear very old baggy cavalry twill trousers, duffle coat and flat cap as he walked round his farms and through his woods. It used to be said with affectionate exaggeration, 'Sir Edmund had only two suits – his "demob" suit and the one he wore to meet the Queen.' He had a charm of manner, which endeared him to all whom he met, treating everyone with the same courtesy, totally devoid of condescension. Yet the more that people came to know him the more surprising and many-faceted character was revealed. Outwardly bluff and genial, able to converse and tell a flow of stories in the broadest Norfolk tongue, for which during their engagement Priscilla said that he must provide a translator, he was at the same time a shrewd business man who often spent half of his week on committees in London. Few of his landowning friends possessed his knowledge of painting, based not on the reading of erudite books about art but on a study of his own inherited collection and on his practice when abroad of heading for the chief galleries as his prime interest. As will become clear, his range of interests was extraordinary but the force which bound his many-sided nature into an impressive unity is less easy to determine. He himself was not given to self-analysis but his deep love of the land, his love of his country, his belief in the importance of continuity and a quiet religious faith combined to enable him to grow into the outstanding East Anglian figure of his generation.

There was nothing soft or superficial about this. He could be alarming at times and many people were afraid of him. His huge frame and his loud voice, almost a bark, was not easily resisted. Timothy Colman has never forgotten Mindy's anger when he had 'poached' the Secretary of the Friends of the Cathedral to stir up and increase the membership of the Norfolk Naturalists' Society. It is curious that such a kindly man never forgot anything which had angered him. The action was forgiven but remained an indelible memory. For any man whom he regarded as not straightforward or fair in his dealings, any whom he termed 'devious' – his worst appellation – there was never forgiveness. Christian charity was never extended to those whom he felt had let him down.

Although he employed an excellent staff at Raveningham consisting of a farm manager and, in early days, three men for every hundred acres, as well as a separate estate staff and two keepers, Mindy was ultimately responsible for the prosperity of the estate. Despite his lack of formal agricultural qualifications, the time spent at Clumber and Coughton had given him sufficient practical experience to enable him to become very knowledgeable. On the farm cereals, freezing peas and sugar-beet were grown. A pedigree dairy herd was kept and a beef unit was maintained. He was well aware of the need to keep abreast of rapidly increasing scientific knowledge and to this end he spent half a day each month at the Norfolk Agricultural Station, then at Sprowston, becoming a member of the executive committee and later succeeding Lord Hastings as chairman. He and his predecessor were between them responsible for developing the Station into the most important experimental farm in existence, specializing in sugar-beet research. In the years that he was also chairman of the British Sugar Corporation his knowledge of the sugar-beet industry was almost unrivalled. It was these two valuable sources of information which were largely responsible for keeping farming methods at Raveningham up-to-date. He felt it imperative to introduce a beet harvester and cleaner for 'it would never do for the Chairman of the Corporation to send too dirty beet to the local factory'. When the Station moved from Sprowston to Wymondham Mindy, against strong opposition, insisted on retaining the land at Sprowston until it was ultimately sold at considerable profit for building development, to the great benefit of the new Station.

Like most of his fellow farmers Mindy was not himself an experimental farmer but in farming, as in many of his other interests, he was an excellent picker of other men's brains, a marvellous asset. He always knew where to get the best advice and he would take it even when it saddened him. He was very fond of his herd of Red Polls; his eye for scenery delighted in the sight of their colour on the landscape. He disliked the black and white British Friesians but when it was pointed out to him by his excellent farm manager, Keith Morgan, that the Red Polls were a considerable economic disadvantage, he knew that sooner or later he must make a change. There was an intermediate stage when he hoped that by the introduction of Red and White Friesians into the dairy herd he might maintain the red cattle; but after fifteen years the lack of accredited pedigree Red and White bulls ended this. The farm had to be a profitable concern, not just a pleasure to the eye. So that he could keep a close watch on his estates Mindy required his estate manager, Geoffrey Wilson, to submit regular accounts of what had been achieved and what was proposed.

Forestry was important both at Raveningham and at Thonock. Mindy managed the 275 acres of Raveningham Woods himself, with the devoted assistance for many years of his forester, George Warnes. When there were special problems to discuss he sought advice from a consultant forester, Edward Garfitt, whom he employed to a much greater extent at Thonock. His principal interest at Raveningham was the growing of high quality oak and sycamore of which he had some exceptionally fine crops. Thanks to his training at Clumber Mindy was a keen and very knowledgeable forester. His uncle, Hickman, had also loved his trees and had always resented the necessity of felling any of them. Local legend maintains that when trees had been marked for felling he would go into the woods, armed with a paint brush and a bucket of whitewash, and alter the markings. During the Second World War, however, the government's need for timber became insatiable and large parts of the 800 acres of Thonock Woods were requisitioned and cut down. After the war, when he had inherited the estate, Mindy was outspoken in his condemnation of the casual way in which his uncle had allowed timber merchants an almost free run of the woods, but Hickman, by then an old man, could do little to save them.

So one of Mindy's early tasks at Thonock was the restoration of the woodland areas. Since many of the remaining trees were over a hundred years old already, in discussion with Garfitt he decided that the trees on the whole area north of the lake in Wharton Wood and Corringham Scroggs must be replaced as rapidly as possible. Garfitt was asked to draw up a plan for this covering a span of thirty years. It was a heavy task. Scrub and choking brambles had first to be cleared away before some 1,700 trees were planted in a season. All available labour was turned on to this and each year a regular pattern of clearance and new planting was established.

Garfitt's advice did not mean any lessening of Mindy's own close watch over what went on his woodlands, especially at Thonock. His minute attention to detail was typical of him. In a letter to Garfitt in January 1978 he wrote: 'I must say that I am a little concerned at the amount of beating up that we seem to have to do [at Thonock]. Comparisons are odious but candidly at Raveningham we do not suffer from this and I think it is possible that one of the reasons is that at Raveningham the men plant in boots, whereas at Thonock I think they plant in rubber boots. I have raised this before and suggested that one tries to get a steel heel which one can clamp over a rubber boot, which obviously makes planting much firmer.'

He was always a kindly and generous landlord but carelessness by a tenant farmer was not treated lightly. There had been a fire in one area of woodland 'due to the stupidity of one of my tenants in allowing burning fertiliser bags to get into the woods. I am not often very vindictive but the Trustees have got to have their full pound of flesh out of this, to see that everything is properly reinstated and compensated for, including the ten years of loss of timber ... I want it to get abroad that if this sort of thing happens then it is going to be very costly from the point of view of those who cause the damage.'

A year or two earlier he had been very dissatisfied with the condition of the timber yard at Thonock, which he had discussed with his estate manager, Geoffrey Wilson. 'I must say I regard it as a complete shambles; timber spread all over the place, long distances to carry it to the benches, and altogether no planning at all ... Some of the timber is full of nails and it would be a mistake to put it on the bench and it should be burnt therefore *in situ* and a better timber should be sorted out and, in my opinion, moved closer to the bench.'

When one of Mindy's regular visits to Thonock coincided with a visit from Garfitt, the two men after a day's tour of the woods settled down for the evening at Ash Villa. Together they went over the forestry plans in detail, with Mindy avid to hear of new ideas, which he discussed with great knowledge and usually without prejudice. However, certain practices he rejected out of hand. He would never tolerate 'line-thinning', the automatic regular removal of whole lines of trees, irrespective of their quality, on the grounds of greater simplicity of management. He greatly disliked the use of chemical weed-killers, thus making the control of planting areas, invaded by birch seedlings, very difficult. Despite the existence of a number of large beech trees along the old Somerby drive he insisted that it was useless to try to grow beech at Thonock. For the most part decisions were not made in a hurry: the same questions would be debated over and over again until he came to a final conclusion. Then no arguments to make him change his mind were accepted. If he thought that he was being thwarted on some matter on which he had made up his mind he could be very angry and he took no care to hide his exasperation. If a disagreement with Garfitt occurred while in the woods he would walk ahead of his companion at great pace in short bursts of energy, a tendency which, after his first heart attack in 1958, worried Priscilla. He very naturally chafed under reminders that he should restrain his desire to walk too fast or too far. Yet to a man whose knowledge he valued and respected, apart from the occasional outburst of pent-up irritation, he was always kind and courteous, for he loved his woods and trees and liked nothing better than to talk about them with an expert, who became a close friend.

Mindy's farming friends in Norfolk seem to have known comparatively little about his much larger Lincolnshire estates. The Thonock and Somerby lands were run as an entirely separate entity. An agricultural scientist, who had sat for over twenty years on committees with him, said that he had seldom heard him mention them. The Lincolnshire scene was very different from that of Norfolk. Apart from the large area of woodland, most of the arable land was held by tenant farmers; Mindy, while keenly interested in the progress of each farm did not himself farm any part of the estate. Living 150 miles away it would have been impossible but he usually managed to visit Thonock each month. Perhaps because he was not directly farming the land himself he was less concerned than he was in Norfolk to introduce labour-saving devices. As late as 1958 a new foreman was surprised to find no motorized transport for his labour force, who still travelled long distances on bicycles and all materials were conveyed by handcart. By the early 1960s this had changed.

In both Norfolk and Lincolnshire Mindy was a greatly revered employer in the old paternalist tradition. It is significant that there was never any trouble with trade unions on his estates. Blessed with an amazing memory he knew all who worked for him, usually by their Christian names, and also their wives and families. In his periodic visits to his Lincolnshire farms he could remember the crops of the previous year, which had shown a good yield and which had been disappointing. 'I love continuity', he often declared and nothing gave him greater pleasure than long service. Some had been with his family for all of their working lives; others had second and even third generation relatives at Raveningham; at Thonock two families have each worked there for over a century.

In consequence his personal care for those who served him was untiring. A letter to the doctor about one who 'has worked for me for well over twenty five years, and consequently I feel very concerned with his welfare' illustrates this. 'He says he is suffering from a duodenal but there is no doubt that in the last few months, in the opinion of all of us who see him constantly, he had gone down hill very rapidly. Yesterday morning he collapsed with a fainting fit and had to be taken home. I have talked to his neighbours and to his brother and there is no doubt in my mind that he is frightened not only of going to doctors and seeing them, but terrified at ever being told by them that he should go to hospital ... I do not know whether he is back at work because this only happened yesterday morning, but if you are passing this way and could look in on him I think it would be a very good thing. If he does come back to work, which I do not think he should do, his dinner hours are 1.00 p.m. to 2.00 p.m. when I think he could be caught at home ... I am very worried about him indeed. I apologise for troubling you but I feel this is the only course to take.'

When a man retired he was never forgotten. Any bereavement in a family was at once followed by a personal letter of sympathy and discreet enquiries about what help might be needed. Once unable to get home from London to snow-bound Norfolk his first questions over the telephone were 'How are the pensioners? Are they all right?' If proof were ever needed that Thonock employees mattered to him as much as those at Raveningham it is found in the fact that on each occasion that one of his children was married a large contingent was transported from Lincolnshire for a memorable day.

It was not all charm; there was never a doubt about who was actively in charge. Accounts regularly submitted to him from the Thonock office were once returned with a slip pinned to them on which was written in red ink 'No names, no pack drill; but somebody doesn't know their job'. He was a good listener to ideas put to him but decision came swiftly and wisely went unchallenged. One tenant farmer, wishing to make changes to the farm buildings, had nervously rehearsed his speech in advance. Only two sentences were delivered before an abrupt 'No' ended the conversation. The foreman, who had decided to liven up the front door of a cottage with a pattern in blue and white paint, was told: 'Do it again. We don't want any seaside nonsense here.'

But all knew exactly where they stood and that he would be absolutely fair with no favouritism. Those at Raveningham naturally knew him best; but he mattered equally to those at Thonock for they mattered equally to him. As one tenant farmer put it, 'I somehow felt better after a visit from Sir Edmund' and another family so much enjoyed his visits of inspection that 'we almost felt offended if he visited another farm and not ours'. Today in inevitably changed circumstances, particularly the Thonock farmers feel that they have lost a leader who, in a sense, was head of their family and they regret the passing of the old order. 'The day I heard Sir Edmund had died', said one at Raveningham, 'was the saddest day of my life.'

In all his devoted work for his estates Mindy had one blind spot. Immensely prodigal of his time for people who needed his help – for people mattered to him above all else – he was not equally prodigal when it came to spending money on the upkeep of farm buildings when he deemed this unnecessary. He could rightly claim great credit for having installed bathrooms into 65 cottages on the estates but those who knew Raveningham and Thonock, whether as workers on the estates or as fellow agriculturalists, are agreed that Mindy tended to run his properties on the smell of an oil rag. The actual farming and the forestry were admirably organized but, with no reflection on his farm managers who were powerless, the farm buildings were not equally well maintained. In Mindy's eyes a coat of paint when essential was all that was needed and he saw no need for a thorough-going regular upkeep. Unfortunately he had no eye for colour and when Priscilla saw a new paint even worse than what it replaced being applied, she intervened and persuaded him to use a pleasant blue. It is strange that the rolling programme of continuous maintenance, which he would later institute for Norwich Cathedral, was never followed at Raveningham. It was a case of penny wise pound foolish. If a cottage or farm building proved to be no longer needed its roof would be removed so as to avoid paying rates and it was allowed to stand derelict. With greater foresight some of the cottages might have become a useful source of income in days when there was an unmet demand for accommodation.

Mindy and Priscilla were tireless hosts. Their guests could range from the Queen Mother or King Olav to county officials, justices of the peace, Yeomanry officers, experts on painting intent on studying his water-colours or anxious to borrow some for an exhibition, clergy, farming experts, university dons and the occasional student. Some who stayed the night in winter might contrast the warmth of their welcome with the cold of the house, for thanks to his austere upbringing Mindy was largely indifferent to heat or cold. Nor did food and drink interest him unduly. Simple food, like his favourite meat pies for shooting lunches or a hunk of cold meat cut off by him from a joint in the kitchen, pleased him best. Creature comforts never ranked high on his list of justifiable expenditure.

While a very large number of people enjoyed Mindy and Priscilla's hospitality, the Hall was never thrown open to the public. The immensely valuable pictures within the house made this a wise precaution. To have a meal or to attend a meeting at the Hall was, as one man put it, like sitting in a room in the National Gallery. On the other hand, the gardens, which Priscilla, victorious over unrewarding soil, supervised with expert devotion, were at certain times open on behalf of various good causes. On these days Mindy retreated to his study, half pulled down the blinds and then stationed Beulah at the window to keep prying visitors at bay, whilst he watched golf or cricket or racing on the television. For a man who in his busy years never went near a racecourse, he had an unexpected knowledge of horses and considerable interest in the breeding of the winners of the classic races.

In another way Mindy acted as a genial host. He was a very keen and good shot, who thoroughly enjoyed the shooting parties which he organized at Raveningham. Two of his guests have described a typical day: 'At breakfast on shooting days Mindy was unapproachable and one did not approach. Bellows for dogs or whatever resounded through the house. Not that he was flapping, far from it, for everything was in control. Bellows were the norm and seemed indeed a kind of soliloquy on the current state of affairs. But he seemed only to become himself again, genial, laughing, anecdotal, when all the guns were safely "embussed".' 'When it was time to set out and Mindy had bellowed to all and sundry "en Voiture", one would climb up into the canvas covered lorry with a selection of guns, which might include a government whip, a judge, an officer R.N. (retd), a farm manager, a frozen food tycoon, somebody's younger son, a senior diplomat, a picture dealer or an equerry. He knew something of the world of each of them and was ready to know more. Nothing in the mixed conversation was more rewarding than to hear a remark capped by one of his shouts of laughter.' To him shooting days should be fun. He always took a back place himself, preferably walking up with the beaters. If you didn't know where he was, pheasants falling dead in the air, followed by a distant report, betrayed his presence.

No pheasants were reared on the estate for he disliked the wholesale slaughter of birds which occurred on some shoots. When his godson, Bamber Gascoigne, who, as a young man, found his godfather a rather formidable figure, wrote a fairy story about pheasants and breeding, the copy presented by the author to Mindy was not well received. It was useless for Gascoigne to explain that the tale was purely imaginary and something of a joke. Mindy did not always share another person's sense of humour. Not that he did not enjoy stories about shooting. He frequently told the story, which he claimed originated at Holkham, about how Lord Leicester shot his gamekeeper. When he went to apologize, the keeper, who was mopping himself up, stood up and said: 'That's all roit, me Lord. Your grandfather shot my grandfather, your father shot my father, and now you've shot me. That's all roit, me Lord.' Mindy expected his guests, who came to shoot, to know the form. One day his son-in-law, Ronald Hoare, and an ambassador were both staying at Raveningham. Accompanied by Mindy and a dog they each took a gun with them as they walked over part of the estate. At one moment they fired at a hare only to be the victims of Mindy's fury. 'I'll never ask you two young men to shoot again.' Neither, and certainly not the ambassador, could be described as a 'young man' and both were utterly at a loss to know how they had offended. The dog had been in no danger of being shot. On asking Mindy to tell them what they had done wrong they learned that the dog was young and only partially trained and might have undone its earlier training by racing, uncommanded, after the hare. Mindy had expected them to know this without having had to be told.

Apart from the care of his own estates Mindy became increasingly involved in fostering agricultural development first in Norfolk and later at national level. His first commitment on returning from the war was membership of the War Agricultural Committee, formed to force farmers to meet the national needs and avoid unnecessary dependence upon imports of food at the mercy of the German U-boats. The surrender of Germany could not immediately relieve the situation and Mindy's powers of persuasion were much in demand to convince East Anglian farmers that government control was likely to continue for some years.

In addition to the Norfolk Agricultural Station, two other Norfolk bodies claimed his help – the Norfolk Chamber of Agriculture and the Royal Norfolk Agricultural Association. The former had existed for over a century but its work was gradually taken over by the County Council and other local government authorities. The Royal Norfolk Agricultural Association was occasionally a fractious body of individualists who, as one critic said, needed dragging into the twentieth century. Here Mindy's determination not to be hidebound by the past was invaluable and a tribute to his success was that he was Chairman of the Association for seven years in the 1970s.

The Royal Norfolk Show was an annual event in which he long played a dominant part. He was President in 1953 when the show was at Raveningham. In a county like Norfolk, out on a limb, an agricultural show is more than a farming occasion; it is a focus of the whole life of a community. On the actual days of the Show his huge height and his loud greeting for countless friends made him a figure whom no one could miss, totally in his element and never thoughtlessly passing anyone by. On the occasion of Royal visits his expertise in what was needed was unrivalled: protocol was strictly observed but in a happily relaxed atmosphere. Behind the scenes officials knew that problems put to him, whether financial or administrative, would be solved quickly and concisely. Having listened carefully to the facts and details about the background, which he invariably knew without needing to be told, he gave his questioner exactly the help which was wanted. One year the secretary of the Show, John Stimpson, was concerned that there could be too many people at lunch on the first day, the prestigious day, and he wanted to move a certain lady to the second day. 'Do just that', said Mindy, 'she's lucky to have an invitation at all.' At the same time he could be stern. Just before his retirement from the Lord Lieutenancy Stimpson, knowing that a successor was under consideration, suggested a name of one who had been much involved with the Show. 'I think we can safely leave that to the Queen, don't you?' A riposte which Stimpson felt was deserved.

Towards the end of his time Mindy was actively concerned with the building of a new pavilion and it was his hope that it might be opened by the Queen, who would lunch there. The luncheon proposal was only possible if the Queen avoided the centre of Norwich in her journey to the Show. Mindy saw no harm in this but the Clerk to the City Council, Gordon Tilsley, pointed out the slight to the City and Mindy yielded. This was the only occasion when, in Tilsley's opinion, Mindy's judgement was at fault in his dealings with the City and was, perhaps, a sign of age but certainly a sign of his love for the Royal Norfolk Show. Despite all his activities at national level and his incredible range of interests, his deepest love was the land. He always upheld his favourite maxim: 'You should live as if you were going to die tomorrow and farm as if you were going to live for ever.' On the occasions of the weddings of his chidren he would, when signing the marriage register, proudly give his occupation as 'Farmer'.

7

Sugar–Beet and Little Neddy 1955–74

Sugar-beet was a relatively new crop in British agriculture. Efforts made in the nineteenth century to establish a prosperous sugar-beet industry had failed. It was the urgent need for home-grown supplies of sugar during the First World War and the subsequent widespread agricultural depression, when the serious threat of starvation was removed and imports again became possible, which together stimulated the establishment of sugar-beet growing and processing in the 1920s as part of the general recovery. In 1935 the government made it a condition of continuing financial support that the several companies running the eighteen sugar factories should amalgamate to form the British Sugar Corporation. Twenty years later Mindy joined the board of the Corporation and early in April 1957 became chairman on the death of Sir Alan Saunders. No one had troubled to ask him if he wanted the post and he only learned of it from the chance remark of a colleague in the train on the way home from Sir Alan's funeral. When the minister, Heathcot-Amory, officially appointed him on 20 May, he assured Mindy that it would only be a two-days-a-week job: it soon proved to be far more demanding for Mindy did a job fully or not at all. Nevertheless, in retirement he maintained that 'the period in my life, which, I think, I enjoyed best of all was Chairman of the old B.S.C.' It was after his time that it became known as British Sugar.

Between his acceptance of the chairmanship and his retirement eleven years later the story of the British Sugar Corporation is one of steady growth, modernization and outstanding success. In his first public statement he promised to visit all eighteen factories at the earliest possible date. To 'meet the troops' in the field was to him his first priority. This was not to be a once-for-all visit for he made it his business as chairman to pay, if humanly possible, an annual visit to each factory. Before long he had come to know personally almost everyone employed by the Corporation and to recall, without prompting, something about their families and their outside interests. As on his farms, his phenomenal memory acted like a tonic, raising morale and stimulating production.

While these visits were prompted by a genuine concern for the welfare of those for whom he felt responsible, there was another purpose in this activity. As chairman he intended to know exactly what was going on everywhere; he asked ceaseless and searching questions and if he were not told correctly or was in some way kept in ignorance there was trouble. Rupert Taylor, Agricultural Director of the Corporation, said that he used to wonder apprehensively, as he heard his Christian name shouted along the corridor, what the chairman was going to ask him. Since the factories existed to produce a foodstuff it was not enough to run a financially sound business; the highest standards of cleanliness must be observed. All employees at all times must wear clean overalls. On the occasion of an inspection of the Cantley processing factory in Norwich he found everything newly painted and spick and span in the area he was expected to visit. He at once demanded to see the employees' lavatories and raised hell at their unsatisfactory condition.

Not only did his inquisitiveness in every aspect of the Corporation's work give him a clear insight into what was happening but the affection which his concern for each employee engendered was at the same time shrewd business. After his retirement there was some industrial trouble. 'That never happened in my time', he remarked. This was true for he made sure that the chairman was not a remote figure but a man to whom the whole workforce mattered. Among his papers he preserved a letter written by one R. R. Fairweather who had worked for many years in the Cantley factory. It was written in capital letters, with the minimum of punctuation, but speaks of the warmth of affection which Mindy aroused in those who worked for him.

Dear Sir, you may wonder who I am well I am the man that have a yarn with you at the Cantley Pensioners Dinner you know I was in the H.M.S. Vindictive at Zeebrugee when we raided the mole I got shrapnel wounds when the Daffodil held us against the mole 1918 well I saw in the paper you were not well and ill and could not attend the Assemble Rooms at Norwich, well I hope these few lines will find you better. As you once told me we are all getting old. I shall be 83 on 11th Jan, if I live that long, as I have not felt all that good lately. Well I hope you find these few lines to be in better health and see another Xmas through. Hope all your family are well all beet sugar factorys seem to be doing well this year so far I spent 40 years at Cantley as a shift electrician allso in the factory Home Guard, spent 17 years in the Navy was at the battle of Faulkland Islands in 1914 we sunk five German warships but they sunk Admiral Craddock on H.M.S. Monmouth and Good Hope and did not pick up one man what a waste of lives still thats war. I spent 3 years in China and Japan on H.M.S. Hawkins. Thats when we had a Navy. Well Sir Happy Xmas and a New Year to you all. May see you next year.

The remarkable growth in the Corporation's profitability was not achieved simply by Mindy's interest in the employees. At the risk of angering shareholders, he insisted that a substantial proportion of the Corporation's profits must be ploughed back into the purchase of the newest machinery. But most of the money for these investments had to be 'earned' under a new incentive agreement, which Mindy regarded as an admirable way of avoiding wasteful expenditure — his deep-seated dislike. 'As we all know', he told the Sugar Club in New York, 'a technician the world over will sell his soul, or anyone else's, for a piece of new equipment. By this means [the incentive agreement] he cannot get new equipment unless he has earned it by past efficiency.'

Early friction with the cane sugar-producing organizations headed by Tate and Lyle ceased when Mindy set up the British Sugar Bureau, an unofficial body which existed to remove unnecessary rivalries and which flourished as a result of his personal friendship with men like Sir Ian Lyle and Sir Peter Runge and from his visits to the West Indies to study their methods. Furthermore, the fame of the British Sugar Corporation spread into Europe. Following a visit by Russian technologists the U.S.S.R. purchased two complete beet sugar factories made in Britain. At first the Russian visitors had refused to believe that so small a work-force could be true and they accused their hosts of hiding men in the fields. From Yugoslavia and Iran young men came to be trained. Challenged on the grounds that mechanization inevitably results in potential unemployment his reply was: 'I do not believe that mechanization is reducing the number of men required by the industry to the extent that people seem to think, for we have got much more diverse in our farming techniques. But it has taken the back-ache out of which were originally pretty unpleasant tasks and I am all for that.'

By 1964 a new deal for shareholders was negotiated with the government, which had given him no support in earlier troubles with the shareholders. Mindy had now judged that the time was ripe to reward those who had supported the British Sugar Corporation for insufficient annual reward. Four years later, on 27 February 1968, he rose to make his final speech as chairman at the annual shareholders' meeting. He was able to point to a great achievement by all concerned: the average yield of beet per acre had increased by 27 per cent; precision drilling had risen from 10 per cent to 85 per cent; mechanical harvesting from 50 per cent to 95 per cent; cleaner-loaders were now used on nearly 60 per cent of the crop; oil fuel was beginning to replace coal and despite the rapid spread of automation 7,000 employees were now needed, of whom 80 per cent were employed all the year round. After his retirement inevitable criticism followed. It was asserted that he had been too close to what went on in the daily routine; that the excellence of his relations with the work-force made him less good in taking overall control of the strategy which a big business enterprise needed. Whatever the truth of this criticism, the figures which he had quoted in 1968 cannot be lightly disregarded. Recognition of his achievement had come in 1965 by his appointment as a Knight of the British Empire.

No less important nationally was his appointment on 1 November

1966 as the first chairman of the Economic Development Committee for the Agricultural Industry, an offshoot of the National
Economic Development Council, familiarly known as 'Neddy'.
Over the years Neddy had spawned twenty 'Little Neddys' to
deal with various aspects of the country's economic problems and
it seems strange that the agricultural Neddy was the 21st to be
formed. As he later told the National Farmers' Union of Scotland
his appointment 'was not without humour. I was summoned one
morning to an imposing building in Whitehall where I was
subjected to considerable pressures to persuade me to accept the
Chairmanship of this Little Neddy. In my ignorance and, I regret
to say, my arrogance, I fondly imagined that this onslaught
was perpetrated to ensure that without question the services of
outstandingly the best man should be secured. The pressures
became obvious and I was properly deflated to read two days later
in a national newspaper – so it must have been true – that no less
than six other gentlemen had been offered the job and had turned
it down flat.' To make his acceptance possible he was released
from being chairman of the Ministry of Agriculture's standing
advisory committee on fertilizers and foodstuffs on which he had
sat since 1950.

The Agricultural Neddy was mainly concerned with the
medium and long-term aspects of the industry. The manpower
situation became a major problem when in 1970 the government
adopted a national policy of agricultural expansion at a moment
when, as Mindy pointed out, 'the decline of hired workers has
been faster than the total decline envisaged for both farmers and
hired workers'. His committee was also instructed to discover
what could be done by 1972 to save imports and what resources
in men and materials would be needed. All of these deliberations
were taking place before Britain's entry into the Common Market,
in which event 'the whole of our thinking will have to be re-
orientated'.

The committee consisted of representatives of farmers, farm
workers, landowners and government departments: Mindy was
not over-optimistic about the outcome of their deliberations. 'No
doubt we shall produce a lot of paper in the process. The last
century was the age of the spoken word, of great political orators
and long sermons. Our century is the age of the written word, of

voluminous reports and long and complicated Acts of Parliament. A friend of mine informed me that he had recently received an official document dealing with the sale and care of cabbages. This had run to over 1280 words. A little research showed him that this exceeded the combined length of the Lord's Prayer, the Gettysburg Speech and Magna Carta.'

Had he thought the work of this 'Little Neddy' useless Mindy would never have accepted the chairmanship. The committee had been formed at a time of a world population explosion, which raised acute problems of feeding. Countries hitherto exporters of foodstuffs now needed the food for their own peoples. To continue to import food which we should be producing ourselves made the situation worse. Furthermore, at home the demand of good farming land for industry, housing, roads, reservoirs and playing fields increased each year the difficulty of growing more food in Britain. When he took over the chairmanship Mindy vividly illustrated the meaning of the spectacular increase in population by referring solely to Britain, not generally regarded as having the same problem as the underdeveloped countries. It was true that in Britain the increase had been less dramatically sudden. 'This year, 1966, is the 900th anniversary of the Battle of Hastings and probably more people than ever will claim descent from William the Conqueror. Are their claims really spurious? I understand that only 25 Knights have been definitely identified by name as having taken part in the battle. Yet 30 generations later their descendants have totalled 25 billion or eight times the present population of the world. From what one hears of the early Knights maybe this is an underestimate! But on this basis who is not descended from the Conqueror?'

Mindy was well aware that his committee by itself could not solve these daunting problems. During the five years of his chairmanship he saw the task of himself and his colleagues as the examination of the whole question of production and distribution of food before too late. Having done this, recommendations for action must be made to the government, which alone could implement their suggestions. This was done in a valuable report made in 1968, which outlined a policy for stabilizing markets and strengthening the confidence of British farmers and horticulturists.

In April 1974 Mindy's outstanding achievements for agriculture were recognized by the award of the Royal Agricultural Society of England's Gold Medal. In acknowledging the award he wrote: 'I must say I never contemplated receiving this award and as it comes for things I really enjoyed doing I must say that I think the lily has been gilded a little too much. I have had a wonderful life and I have enjoyed practically everything that has come my way and to be given a Gold Medal on top of this seems to be a little bit unfair.'

8

In the City

Those with little knowledge of Mindy's full life sometimes fondly imagined that he spent most of his time dancing attendance on members of the Royal Family when they visited Norfolk. They would have had no idea that more often than not he was in London on two or three days each week for meetings of his family property company, the Colville Estate, of Lloyds Bank or the Eastern Board of the Transport Commission, of the Church Commissioners and, above all, of 'Little Neddy' and the British Sugar Corporation. Those who knew of his multifarious activities might well argue that the management of the Raveningham and Thonock estates and, after 1949, the duties of the Lord Lieutenancy were sufficiently time-consuming to keep him in East Anglia but he himself had no doubt that 'exertions confined solely to any part [of the country] are likely to be stultifying'. Of course, he was always doing too much but 'after all, who is not, who is worth anything at all in these days?' Moreover, he greatly enjoyed his City life. A directorship of Lloyds Bank meant membership of a congenial body, almost another club. Frequent visits to London provided an excuse to go to his favourite dining club – Pratt's – where a special chair was earmarked as 'his' and where he would sit, surrounded by friends, listening to their 'shop' and telling his familiar stories in the broadest of Norfolk accents.

One story which he loved to tell was, like any good story, not only current in Norfolk.

A visitor to a Norfolk church found there an old man, who was clearly both a kind of caretaker and an institution. The two got talking and the visitor said 'You must have seen a great many changes in your time and known a lot of Rectors'. 'Aah', said the old man, 'oi 'av that, shure n'ough. Rectors they coom and they goo. O'ive seen 'en arl and they've arl see'd me. One there was, a Naval Gentleman 'e were. 'E calls me a Sextant. Arter 'im we 'ad Rector oo loiked butterflois and moths and the loik. 'E calls me a Beetle. Then there were an oigh church Gentleman. Very oigh 'e were; one of these 'ere Angular-Catholics oi reckon they call 'em. 'E dressed me oop in a lidl woit frock and called me a Vaargin.

These stories and the manner of telling them were famous. Mindy had not been an actor for nothing. But stories could be told anywhere and London meant more to Mindy than a pleasant evening. 'When a man is tired of London he is tired of life.' Mindy would have fully endorsed Dr Johnson's opinion, for London gave him the intellectual stimulus, less easily available in Norfolk, which he needed.

He joined the board of the Colville Estate Ltd in 1930 and when Hickman died in 1945 he succeeded him as chairman, a post which he held until 1977, thereafter remaining as a director until he died. Hickman, quite apart from his collection of water-colours and his engaging eccentricities, had been a remarkably shrewd and generous chairman, in virtual control of the company during the war years when few directors were free to attend meetings. Mindy took over the chairmanship at a difficult time, having to face the frustrating problems of post-war reconstruction of damaged or destroyed property when labour and materials were in very short supply. It was necessary to take a firm grip of the company's affairs. Quarterly board meetings now took the place of the war-time annual formal approval of the accounts and the rather narrow family domination of the board was broadened by the help of men of wider business experience like E. F. O. Gascoigne and Mark Strutt of the firm of Strutt and Parker, who, although a director since 1940, could only become involved after his return from active service. At the same time the character of the company as very much a Bacon family concern was maintained.

On Hickman's death Mindy had inherited the Chancery Lane property, the original 'fields' given to the Lord Keeper by Queen Elizabeth I. He could jest about 'farming part of Chancery Lane' but his inheritance meant heavier demands for death duty than he could meet and, despite war damage claims, the rehabilitation of the property was another serious financial burden. Understandably, he was reluctant to sell land which had been in his family for nearly four centuries and in 1948, on the suggestion of Gascoigne, he transferred the whole Chancery Lane property to the Colville Estate in return for an agreed sum of money and a free issue of shares, dividends on which would only begin to be payable when rehabilitation was complete. At the time this was regarded as a fair settlement and Mindy was pleased to feel that he had maintained the family ownership.

While the acquisition of the Chancery Lane property greatly enhanced the company's prospects, the years that followed brought the need to take many far-reaching decisions about the sale of outworn buildings and investment in new property to replace them. Although some directors feared that Chancery Lane would not prove to be a potentially valuable area in the City, it gradually became apparent that it had been wise to retain the Lord Keeper's 'fields' rather than to seek for property solely outside London. Thanks in no small measure to Mindy's unremitting interest in the company and his care for the shareholders, all concerned began to profit handsomely. New properties in Reigate and Sheffield testified to the company's successful growth and shortly before his death Mindy approved property investment in the United States and especially in California. Queen Elizabeth I's shrewd Lord Keeper would have approved of his descendant.

Mindy became a director of Lloyds Bank in February 1950 under the chairmanship of Lord Franks. At that time directors were chosen both for their business skills and also for their influence in their particular part of the country. Thus when in 1951 it was decided to form subsidiary regional boards Mindy was the obvious choice as the first chairman of the Eastern Counties Regional Board, which had its headquarters in Cambridge where he presided over fortnightly meetings. He remained a director until 1973, also serving on three of the bank's London committees dealing with staff problems and also with premises and general development. As a gregarious man he thoroughly enjoyed the regular meetings and the excellent lunches which followed. He could not fairly be described as a financial wizard but he was, like his uncle Hickman, a sound man of business. At board meetings he did not speak overmuch but his contributions to discussions were wise and he was listened to with respect. At one time there were suggestions that he might become vice chairman but he did not wish this since he would not have been able to give the amount of time which he felt would be necessary.

In the years when he was also chairman of the British Sugar Corporation he had become very friendly with Sir Eric Faulkner then chairman of Glynn, Mills & Co. and he would often come and get advice about the Corporation's finances. When Faulkner became chairman of Lloyds Bank in 1969 he was glad to work closely with Mindy and to respect his judgement. Distinguished fellow directors and senior bank executives alike admired his common sense and highly valued his friendship. It was not an easy time for any bank. Faulkner was anxious to make Lloyds an international bank, a great change from previous policy. In addition, during the decade 1961–71 there had been only 26 months during which banks were free from some form of quantitative or qualitative control on their lending. Difficult times brought growing inter-bank competition and rivalry, demanding new ideas and methods. In 1969 Lloyds pioneered the introduction of cheque cards and the first cash dispensers were installed. The Access credit card followed in 1971. When in the following year Britain entered the E.E.C. a new range of problems and opportunities was opened. As a director Mindy was closely involved with all these developments.

It would be wrong to claim that he was pesonally responsible for initiating the policy followed by Lloyds in the years that he was a director. What can be claimed is that at Lloyds, as in all of his other activities, once he was convinced after careful study and thought that change was in the bank's best interests he supported it wholeheartedly and with no backward-looking regrets. Because he was always aware of the danger of not moving with the times, he believed that a retirement age of 70 was wise. Although many men, not least himself, have much to contribute after that age, others have lost their vitality and can be retired without any ill-feeling. Not all the directors shared this view and on the Eastern Counties Regional Board he had trouble with Lord Butler in 1972, who had been appointed without reference to him, and who now strongly objected to retirement at 70. Mindy was adamant that there could be no exceptions made to the rule. In the end, although Butler was four months his senior, Mindy offered to retire at the same time.

Being specially concerned with staff welfare, Mindy had always taken great pains to ensure the appointment and, where justified, the advancement of good, younger men for the chief positions and he believed that bank officials would not feel complete confidence in the directors if they outstayed their time. There had long been a tradition of holding church services for Lloyds officials but, with his usual common sense, he wrote in 1971 to Faulkner to say that he and others felt that these services had outlived their original purpose. 'The main reason, however, why we feel they should go is that they are really a farce. We are convinced that the majority come because they feel that it will probably be noticed if they are not there and this might have a detrimental effect on their futures. We feel that this is not the best attitude for coming to Services like this.'

After retirement in 1973 Mindy kept up his connections with his former fellow directors. This was not an attempt to hold on to the post but an enjoyment of meeting with old friends. A letter referring to the retired directors' annual lunch makes this clear. 'I have firmly booked the 13 November in my diary and it will be either death or a serious illness that will keep me from lunching on that day.' Michael Falcon, a trustee of Mindy's estate and a director of Lloyds, recalls Mindy's enjoyment of these occasions. On the drive to Cambridge Mindy would ask searching questions about all the people who had served the bank in his day. Falcon believes that usually Mindy knew the answers already and was testing him to see if he was taking the right interest in the welfare of the bank's employees. After Mindy's first serious heart attack in 1958 his doctor advised against drinking port or brandy at the end of the regular directors' lunches: he suggested drinking kümmel as a safer alternative. As a result at every lunch kümmel was passed round. When this happened at one of the retired directors' lunches, Mindy turned to Falcon and said with obvious pleasure, 'I see that they haven't forgotten me!' He also decided on his doctor's advice that he should give up some of his directorships, including that of the British Rail Eastern Division, meetings of which lasted from 9 a.m. until 6 p.m.

Mindy's business connections brought him a wide range of friends and acquaintances in the City and to a lesser extent at Westminster, though he never sought to play any part in politics. Apart from the pleasure which he derived from this, it meant that he knew the right people to approach for advice and help in any project. Although not strictly part of the business side of his career, it is justifiable to include at this point the story of his unfailing support of his old friend, Sir Humphrey Gibbs, who had become Governor of Rhodesia in 1959 and who on 11 November 1965 faced an unprecedented situation when Ian Smith announced the country's Unilateral Declaration of Independence from the British Commonwealth. Mindy's knowledge of key figures in the City and in the Colonial Office was to prove invaluable.

For the next four years Gibbs was to remain to all intents and purposes isolated in Government House in Salisbury. A virtual boycott was imposed and his salary ended by Smith's illegal regime. Mindy was acutely distressed the more he learned of his friend's plight. For the moment there was only one thing which he could do to give immediate comfort and that was to fly to Rhodesia to spend a week in January 1966 in Government House. His cheerful presence lessened the sense of isolation and Mindy was enabled to assess in what ways more permanent help could be given. He encouraged Gibbs to continue to go to his club in Salisbury where Mindy had the slightly embarrassing experience of being caged in a lift, which had temporarily broken down, with Ian Smith as companion. What worried Mindy most was the certainty of an ever-increasing strain on Gibbs's personal finances as long as he remained at Government House responsible for its upkeep.

Everything turned on how long Gibbs felt in honour bound to represent his Sovereign in Rhodesia. Lord Malvern, Prime Minister for nearly a quarter of a century of Southern Rhodesia and later of the Federation of Rhodesia and Nyasaland, told Mindy during this first visit that he believed that the Government should release Gibbs soon. On his return seeking advice from Faulkner about Gibbs's financial difficulties, Mindy wrote: 'His sense of duty is such that I know only too well that if they tell him he should stay on then I have no doubt that he will agree to. Anyway the politicians of this country of either party will always use him for their own interests without any regard to the strain it imposes on him.' By April 1968 Mindy was writing to Gibbs's elder brother: 'I do myself feel that this farce really ought to be brought to an end by the Government. I think it is really asking too much and as usual they are not concerned with the effect that their dilatoriness has on individuals. I know a lot of people feel that it is a great advantage having Humphrey there, maybe it is, but I really think they are asking an awful lot of him ... If this strain continues I shall have to try to get out and see him again.' He had already paid a second visit in January 1967 and, despite very heavy duties as Lord Lieutenant 'with three Royal visits coming off before the end of June' he somehow managed to fly to Salisbury for a final visit late in June 1969.

He undertook this journey in very poor health. In addition to the need of avoiding undue strain on his heart, he had had serious trouble with a duodenal ulcer and his doctor had urged him to rest in bed. This advice he felt bound to disregard; the sole concession which he made was to travel first class on the plane against his usual practice. Despite messages to Salisbury asking that he be allowed to rest on arrival, he plunged straight into a high-powered conference on the future of Rhodesia and its Governor. At no time was he an emissary of the government. 'I certainly did not go out as a delegate and did not go out empowered to offer H.V.G. money from H.M.G.' He always insisted that he came as a personal friend and for this reason, although in touch with the Colonial Office before leaving, he had been careful to avoid seeking an interview with the Prime Minister, Harold Wilson. Although he had strongly disclaimed any official position it had actually been suggested to him at the Colonial Office that if, as was a possibility, a settlement could be reached by means of a new constitution for Rhodesia he might care to draft it and

that the Minister would later come to Salisbury for the final
negotiations. Mindy bluntly pointed out that he was not a lawyer
and that he had no intention of doing the Minister's work for
him. The long and frustrating negotiations between Wilson and
Ian Smith are fully documented in Command Paper 3159: they
are not part of Mindy's story. Throughout the four years 1965 to
1969 he acted solely as Gibbs's personal friend and a staunch friend
and advisor he proved to be.

During his first two visits Mindy had tried hard to persuade
Gibbs to accept a grant from the British Government to reimburse
him for the enforced expenditure which he had incurred consequent upon his remaining at Government House. This Gibbs had
resolutely refused, insisting that he was not going to be placed
under any obligation to the Government. Mindy's final visit
occurred at the moment when the referendum on whether Rhodesia should remain a member of the Commonwealth was being
taken. On the morning of the day on which the result was due
to be announced Mindy wrote to the Vice-Chancellor of the
University of East Anglia apologizing for his absence from the
next Council meeting. 'Today is the big day which will settle
Humphrey Gibbs' future. I am not sanguine as to the result. As
is normal there has been, I fear, too much wishful thinking and
Smith has been built up into a virtual Messiah with all the dangers
that go with that. Anyway I am glad I came as I am sure it has
helped. Interesting but sad times I fear. I did not know that so
many people could be so stupid!'

The result of the referendum, announced on 20 June 1969,
showed beyond any doubt that there was no no further purpose
in Gibbs remaining as Governor. It had been his practice Sunday
by Sunday at 7 a.m. to go to the Cathedral at Salisbury where he
sat in his official pew at the front. Here Mindy had often sat with
him. On the Sunday after the announcement that Rhodesia would
leave the Commonwealth Mindy pointed out that Gibbs should
no longer sit at the front but that the two of them should sit in
one of the pews at the back. This brought home to many Rho-
desians for the first time the breaking of ties with Britain.

Mindy could now press Gibbs even more strongly to accept
financial recompense from the British government. When Gibbs
remained adamant in his refusal Mindy argued that he was being

unfair to his family and that, if only for their sakes, he should accept the sum of money for which he was out of pocket from lack of salary and the ending of all the benefits which a Governor was entitled to enjoy. Eventually Gibbs agreed to Mindy's final plea that a trust should be set up for the benefit of his wife and sons but one from which he himself was excluded. In a memorandum dated 2 November 1970 Mindy wrote: 'This decision was not taken until after he had decided to retire from the post of Governor [and] is something of which I have first hand knowledge. I believe it is true to say that I was the one who persuaded him to agree to allow me to make the approach to the U.K. Government after I had returned to this country, by which time his retirement from the post of Governor had been made public for well over ten days.'

In August 1969 Gibbs and his wife returned to England and were at once invited by the Queen to stay at Balmoral. In recognition of their outstanding services to Rhodesia he was appointed G.C.V.O. and a Privy Councillor, while Lady Gibbs was made a Dame of the British Empire. The four previous years had been a great strain on both of them but Mindy was able to tell Sir Denis Greenhill at the Foreign Office that Lady Gibbs had assured him that 'Sir Humphrey is pretty well. He has just given up smoking and as he used to smoke 60 plus a day this is really quite an achievement!'

It was no light task which Mindy had undertaken. He was greatly assisted on the financial side by advice from Sir Eric Faulkner and by Linklaters and Paine, the solicitors acting for the Gibbs family, who were equally helpful. The situation was further complicated, once a sum of money had been agreed, by a threatened demand for income tax by the Rhodesian government levied on the settlement. In January 1972 Mindy wrote to the lawyers: 'I am quite certain that Sir Humphrey is not in a position to pay Rhodesian tax on this sum should this be levied . . . Further I must ask how are the costs of setting up this Settlement to be met? . . . Again, I am quite certain that Sir Humphrey would not be in a position to meet these costs himself and I hope he will not be asked to. While obviously I cannot be of any assistance on the legal side of the Settlement, I think I can and should draw attention to Sir Humphrey's circumstances at the present time, which I know are not easy.' A week earlier he had written to Gibbs's son about Smith's ambivalent remarks concerning the income tax threat. 'I do not trust Smith a yard and I suspect that it is the cheese-paring attitude of H.M.G. that may well make them not expedite things in the hope that he [Smith] may pay up eventually what he promised.' Thanks to a personal interview with the then Foreign Secretary, Sir Alec Douglas-Home, he was comforted by an assurance that if necessary the Government would meet the income tax demand.

At last the task was over. At the end of March 1973 Mindy could write to the lawyers: 'It is settled and to all who have participated to make it possible I am extremely grateful as the one who, I suppose, really started the thing rolling in Salisbury the day after the result of the Referendum was announced.' He had been a good friend. Yet even now he did not feel that his task was fully completed. He was concerned with the position of the leading members of Gibbs's official household in Salisbury, although this did not present as difficult a problem as had Gibbs himself. His comptroller, Sir John Pestell, his A.D.C. Captain Christopher Owen and his confidential secretary Mrs Belle Baxter, had continued to receive their salaries after U.D.I. but were now subject to heavy income tax demands from the Rhodesian government and might well need help in securing new employment. During 1974 Mindy kept up the pressure on all who could help and thanks to his efforts their loyal service was recognized with grants and their income tax payments reimbursed to them.

Four years later Gibbs took part in a television programme about which Mindy wrote to him: 'You came over extremely well, if I may say so, in the B.B.C. programme on Panorama called "Majesty" and did your stuff admirably. I don't suppose you saw the programme. It was quite good and of course they produced a lot of people who were anti-Monarchy: Willie Hamilton, M.P. for Fife; Whitlam, the sacked P.M. of Australia ... Altrincham, who you may remember was extremely rude about the Queen when he was a silly young man and appears to have learned a little sense but not much; Alec Home, who did well on the pro-side; but on the whole I thought it was pretty fair and anyway you did your stuff to enhance the Monarchy.' This mattered more than all else to Mindy.

9

Town and Gown 1945–82

One of the most striking things about Mindy was the incredible range of his activities and interests. The sheer volume of the work involved makes it difficult for lesser mortals to understand how one man could accomplish so much. Moreover, he would never become associated with an institution or an organization unless he gave himself wholeheartedly to its welfare. He is said to have been the only man to have refused an invitation to become a director of the Norwich Union on the grounds that he could not give sufficient time to its affairs. Had he lived in the eighteenth century he would have been described as 'a man of bottom', a phrase implying the security which landowning wealth then gave, allied to the wisdom gained from experience: at the height of his powers he would have won the admiration of the ancient Romans as a man possessing *gravitas*. Norfolk gained immeasurably from his restless search for fulfilment, a search pursued not by a light-weight who flitted restlessly from one project to another as the fancy took him but by a man with his feet planted firmly on solid ground. The financial security that came from his inheritance, his farming and his City and other interests enabled him to devote thirty-five years of his life to the good of Norwich and Norfolk.

Part of his secret lay in his fascination with people and his insatiable curiosity about the ways in which they earned their living and how they filled their days. He was a great reader and it is not surprising that, apart from the occasional Dick Francis thriller, biographies were his favourite reading; he loved to discover what made famous people 'tick'. He devoured Whitaker's Almanack for accurate facts and figures. Constant questioning of all with whom he came into conduct, allied to a retentive memory, gave him a width of knowledge and understanding invaluable in all his different undertakings. He was never in any sense an intellectual and he disclaimed any scholarly ability. Once at a dinner party when some academics were parading their specialized learning he disarmingly commented, 'Of course, I am only a country bumpkin'. Nothing was further from the truth. The range of his interests and the considerable expertise which he had acquired from his penetrating probing, together with a common sense described by Lord Franks as 'amounting almost to genius', combined to make him the man to whom people turned instinctively for help and advice. In every cause which he supported he was the natural leader.

When recalling all that he did for his county it must be remembered that for twenty-nine years he was its Lord Lieutenant. The voluntary work recorded in this chapter was in no sense part of his Lieutenancy duties, which were quite separate and demanding. At the same time it was without question valuable for the institutions which he served to have the benefit of his position in the county.

Although Mindy never employed a personal private secretary, there was always secretarial help at hand. At Raveningham the farm secretary was available to type other letters for him; secretaries were provided by the British Sugar Corporation and 'Little Neddy'; the Clerk to the County Council who was also the Clerk to the Lieutenancy relieved him of much routine business. Even so, it needed a man able to organize his time well and who enjoyed being busy to keep abreast of all the work involved.

Although in no sense a musician, Mindy in 1949 became President of the historic Norwich and Norfolk Triennial Festival at a moment when it appeared that financial difficulties threatened its continued existence. For a quarter of a century he fostered its revival; one of many examples of his readiness to devote himself to a cause or an institution which he had become convinced was of value to the county, even if not necessarily of prime interest to him personally. But he declined an invitation to be President of the Bach Society, feeling that this office should be held by a musician.

His skill as a reconciler and peacemaker was early tested over the future of the valuable City and County archives. A new City librarian, appointed in 1951, discovered that his most serious problem, requiring immediate action, was the care and administration of the archives, then housed in a rambling and decaying building. The proper care of fragile documents was being made impossible by the intransigent attitude of the County Council towards the equally stubborn City Council. Despite huge arrears of sorting and listing and totally inadequate accommodation, the City Council was unwilling to provide the additional funds needed by the Public Libraries Committee to look after the documents on the grounds that in any case many of the documents dealt with the County and not the City. For its part the County Council had no intention of funding a new archives service either on its own and certainly not in partnership with the City. It was at this juncture that the active Norfolk Records Society gave formal notice that in two years' time they would withdraw their deposits from the Central Library's inadequate strong room, although being expected to give five years' notice of such action.

Somehow this ludicrous deadlock had to be broken. Not only was Mindy genuinely interested in the history of his County but he was always anxious to unite City and County authorities in a common purpose. The first stage was to persuade the conflicting parties at least to meet. A judicious policy of knocking one or two heads together and of pouring oil on troubled waters had its effect. Within a year all in any way concerned with the problem had agreed to meet with the clear aim of producing a scheme which would co-ordinate the efforts of all who were interested in the archives. Five years later the solution was in sight. It had been agreed that a new Central Library was essential and Mindy had quietly persuaded the new Clerk to the County Council to reach agreement with the City about this. In October 1957 it was decided that there should be a Joint Record Office for the City and the County to be housed in the new library. This rather obvious solution came just in time to enable the architect to provide 12,000 square feet of storage strong room in place of the 4,000 originally thought sufficient. Thus thanks in no small measure to Mindy's firm diplomacy Norfolk and Norwich manuscripts and printed sources share one centrally-sited building. Having achieved this he did not lose interest and he continued to find time to attend many meetings of the Norfolk and Norwich Records Committee.

THE RAVENINGHAM PICTURES

Archives were important but not so close to Mindy's heart as were pictures. Thus it was an enjoyable task to be associated with the Norwich Museum and Gallery with its fine collection of works by the Norwich School of artists. It was here that a lasting friendship with a young Assistant Curator, Francis Hawcroft, began. The relationship started slightly embarrassingly. Together they were examining a Constable painting recently acquired by the Curator. 'What do you think of it?', Mindy bluntly demanded, 'to me it's not right'. It was not easy for a young man to pass judgement on his superior's acquisition. However, Mindy proceeded to give Hawcroft detailed reasons why he felt that the painting had been wrongly attributed and he was proved right. Hawcroft, who later became Principal Keeper at the Whitworth Art Gallery in Manchester, has never forgotten the support which Mindy, as a member of the Museum Committee, gave him, when as yet untried, at the start of his career.

Until Hickman had died there was no absolute certainty that his possessions would pass to Mindy: his will could have been altered at any time. Although never a collector himself Mindy's knowledge of the whereabouts of most of the relevant family portraits was considerable. He did purchase a few of these and towards the end of his life acquired the magnificent self-portrait of Sir Nathaniel Bacon. The pictures at Raveningham, broadly speaking, fall into three separate groups. First, there are the family portraits, which include a head and shoulders portrait of Sir Francis Bacon. Then there is the Hickman collection of some four hundred water-colours and drawings, built up by him between about 1880 and 1910. Lastly, there are a number of fine oil paintings, which came from different sources but in the main from John Staniforth Beckett, from whom Hickman inherited them.

To inherit such pictures was a joy but also a heavy responsibility and often a laborious task. Mindy had never received any formal training in art appreciation but he possessed a very good eye for pictures and he cared greatly about the proper care and pres- ervation of his own, for which he always regarded himself as a trustee. By careful study of his own collection and, true to form, by picking the brains of the stream of experts from galleries, museums and private houses, who came to Raveningham to study particular works or to borrow some for an exhibition, he became very knowledgeable. Any expert who queried the attribution of a water-colour was made to write in pencil on the back of the mount the name of the artist whom he thought had done the work and then to sign it. His own taste was apt to be conventional and he particularly enjoyed Dutch landscapes: for modern art he had no great sympathy.

While ready to welcome all who genuinely wished to see and study a picture, he never opened the house to the public, because – as he wrote – 'my only worry is that large crowds on the staircase, which has no support other than being, so to speak, clocked into the side wall, might end in disaster. Added to which the upstairs rooms, I doubt, are really capable of bearing much weight.' More- over, the house was not big enough to open the main rooms to the public and to retain somewhere private. He enjoyed showing his pictures to those able to appreciate them. Dr Alan Borg, then in charge of the Sainsbury Centre for Visual Arts at the University of East Anglia, remembers well what Mindy described as 'a brief look at my pictures'. At the end of two hours only those hanging on walls had been inspected; the water-colours and drawings, for the most part carefully stored in presses, had not been reached.

If understandably he was unwilling to risk opening his house to the public, he was always a very generous lender to exhibitions. This involved a great deal of work for him as he never employed a secretary with sufficient professional knowledge of the collection to act on his behalf. The loan of a single picture might involve half- a-dozen letters, for questions of transport, insurance, photography and care, especially of water-colours easily harmed by exposure to excessive light, had to be organized. As he grew older he came to resent this tedious work as a letter of March 1980 to Alan Borg makes clear.

Dear Alan,

What a bore you are!! I do not know why it is but as time goes on whenever one is asked to lend pictures one is asked to produce more and more detail till one gets completely exasperated and I begin to wonder whether I shall, very shortly, give up lending altogether. However with the University of East Anglia it is somewhat different although the paper [work] is just as intense as it is with everyone else and, in fact, more so.

There are two things that I want to make clear before I get down to the actual pictures. The first is that I have absolutely no idea of their value and therefore I am afraid that you will have to put a value on them and refer this back to me for my approval. The second thing is, and this is something that nearly drives me round the bend, I always lend pictures with existing hooks, wires or chains with them and when they come back I expect them to be sent back with the appurtenances still intact. I know this is a bore for you but you have other people to help you which I do not and this, I am afraid, is a condition.

I sound in a very bad temper this morning but I do not know why; there has been a spate of requests for borrowing pictures and I get rather fed up with having to do all the work myself. However, there it is. Having now blown my top now forget it and here is what you want, I hope.

What Mindy increasingly disliked was the way that organizations like the British Council and the Arts Council were inclined to include his pictures in long tours both in this country and abroad. It also irritated him that some of their experts were prone to save themselves trouble by referring to old exhibition catalogues when making their selection rather than choose something new from his collection. John Gaze, whom Mindy respected as a great Turner expert and who had been in the Fine Arts Department at the University of East Anglia, had been given the unenviable task of approaching him on behalf of the Arts Council in order to borrow some of his finest water-colours for a tour of

China. The answer came in a letter of July 1981: 'I am afraid I am not prepared to allow the *Blasted Oak* by John Crome to leave this country. This drawing is extremely fragile and was in the Tate Gallery basements on loan from my uncle, Sir Hickman Bacon, when the Thames came over and flooded the lower part of the Gallery. This as you can imagine did the drawing no good at all ... Also I am not prepared to lend *View on the Wharf near Farnley* by Thomas Girtin. This is one of the most famous Girtins in existence and, candidly, I think it had better wait, before a drawing of this quality is sent half-way across the world, until the Chinese have got a proper appreciation of watercolour drawings. After all, the appreciation of watercolours is a very sophisticated taste and one could hardly expect the Chinese, who have little experience of British Art, to straight away relish the niceties of the difference between a really great drawing and another one perhaps not of the same quality.'

What is not included in this letter is the fact that the previous exhibition of English water-colours sent to China was that of works by Durham miners. Mindy had no disrespect for this. He merely wished to point out to Gaze that Girtin would not be said to be the next natural step in water-colour appreciation.

In September 1980 the Director of the Tate Gallery, who was arranging a Gainsborough exhibition, received Mindy's reply to his request for a loan. 'As regards *Bumper*, he always seems to be away on loan and therefore it is with some reluctance that I acceed to your request .,. While I am perfectly happy to lend to the Tate, candidly my experiences of lending to France have not been particularly happy. I have found that the French, while they take all good care with the pictures when they arrive at the exhibitions, are inclined once the exhibition is over to bundle them up and send them back and on two occasions I have had pictures damaged in this way. Also it is rather a tall order to be invited to spend from October 7 1980 until April 1981 [away from here].'

One of the most exciting discoveries among his pictures was a small painting of *St Jerome*, which hung in his and Priscilla's bedroom, placed so that they could admire it from bed. David Carritt, the art historian, became interested in the picture when he saw a photograph of it in the Courtauld Institute. When later recounting the story to the press, he told how he took the painting to London in one of Priscilla's shopping bags and entrusted it to the care of a Dr Hell, an expert cleaner. As Mindy later told the Director of the Fitzwilliam Museum Cambridge: 'As you know it was attributed to Carrotto until David Carritt ... got suspicious and felt that there was some connection with the lion and the Dürer lions in Berlin. At any rate, in due course it came to be accepted ... by quite a distinguished number of art critics as a work by this great master. Various other attributions have been made, among them Altdorfer, Cranach and also Hans Baldung. I am no expert but I am pretty certain it cannot be by the first. Absolutely certain that it cannot have been by the second, and having seen it hang alongside another Baldung I would think this is very doubtful.' No expert perhaps, but a man with a remarkable knowledge of and feeling for a picture. The cost of insuring the only painting by Dürer in private hands in this country made it impossible to keep at Raveningham. Priscilla, who had loved the picture, wished that it had not proved to be so valuable. It is now on loan to the Fitzwilliam Museum.

The future of the collection worried Mindy from time to time. In 1976 talk about the possibility of a wealth tax led him to explore the idea of giving part of the collection to an overseas museum or, perhaps, to a university in New Zealand. Fortunately this proved unnecessary but his thinking on the project remains interesting. In a letter to a tax consultant on heritage problems he wrote: 'What put this idea into my mind was the possibility of the effect of a wealth tax on collections of pictures. I have always regarded myself as a trustee of any collections which have come down to me. If a wealth tax was to be levied on pictures then the only way in which one could find the money would be to sell a picture from time to time to provide the necessary cash. This would, of course, have the effect of destroying the collection. Our own museums are already full to overflowing of good works of art, which cannot possibly be shown and repose in the cellars. My idea, therefore, was to give them abroad to some museum who would be glad to display them. Added to which, one might well feel that if this country wished, by legislation, to destroy deliberately collections that have been made, one would take action as far as one could oneself to avoid this possibility.'

He regarded it as quite understandable that, if he were ever to sell any pictures, the Fitzwilliam should be very interested in acquiring the Dürer and the National Gallery equally anxious to acquire the Brouwer *Tavern Scene*, loaned to the Gallery by Hickman in about 1907. However, a letter written early in 1981 makes clear that as far as he was concerned he hoped to keep the collection intact. 'I have always regarded myself and shall always regard myself as a Trustee of this collection. I am 78 and therefore coming to the end of my life and it is my intention to leave all the works of art that I possess – most of which, particularly the pictures that have already been exempted from State Duty as it was then and which I hope will be exempted in the future – to my son, Nicholas. I am thankful to think that he takes a great interest in the collection and will therefore not do anything hasty with it ... I would hope that he will be able to keep it intact by some means or other.'

The Dürer remains in Cambridge, largely for safe keeping. The Brouwer, which had been for eighty years with the National Gallery, was brought back to Raveningham early in 1987. Nicholas felt that it was time for it to come home.

Two institutions, one beginning its life in 1963 and the other dating from some forty years after the Battle of Hastings, occupied much of Mindy's time over many years. The University of East Anglia and the Cathedral Church of the Holy and Undivided Trinity of Norwich both owed a deep debt of gratitude to his constant care and interest and to his clear vision.

THE UNIVERSITY OF EAST ANGLIA

The 1950s and 60s were years marked by an unparalleled expansion of university education in Britain and Norwich was chosen as the natural centre for a university serving the needs of East Anglia. The original hope had been to acquire a bombed site within the City but this proved too costly and cramped so the first 113 students began their university life at Earlham, some four miles from the City centre. The promotion committee, under the chairmanship of Lord Mackintosh, had been determined to found a truly modern university, which would not be a pale reflection of

Oxford and Cambridge either in its aims and purpose or its architecture. The majority on the committee believed that it should be a secular institution with no theological faculty and no formal provision for organized religion. This presented the first Vice-Chancellor, Professor Frank Thistlethwaite, with the delicate task of steering an aceptable course between the opposition of most of his academic colleagues to any kind of religious presence on the campus and the wishes of influential Norfolk figures, to whom the University looked for financial support, who disliked the total exclusion of all religious activities.

Mindy was not a member of the promotion committee. His direct involvement in the affairs of U.E.A. began in 1964 when, on the death of Lord Mackintosh, he became Pro Chancellor and the first Chairman of Council. Unlike many of the leading East Anglian figures he had the ability to understand the needs of a modern university. His own brief university career prevented him from being hidebound by the traditional academic subjects and from the early days of U.E.A. he campaigned strongly for the University to have a high grade business school, as was common to many American colleges. He was apt to get his own way on matters about which he felt strongly but unfortunately he proved too far-sighted on this proposal. He did, however, with some difficulty persuade the University Council to support an outstanding Fine Arts Department. The John Innes Institute devoted to agricultural research was more easily supported in a county like Norfolk and became another source of strength to the University.

The early years of the University were far from easy and it has been said that in no small measure it was Mindy's strength which kept it from falling apart. Success was also due to the partnership of Pro Chancellor and Vice Chancellor. Professor Frank Thistlethwaite came to Norwich from a Fellowship at St John's College in Cambridge, bringing with him a wealth of new ideas and a readiness to build the University upon new and largely untried lines. As a sensitive man he relied frequently upon what he called Mindy's rock-like support when the going got rough. Mindy could ride out a storm more easily than Thistlethwaite but he had not the experience to provide the academic impetus. U.E.A. owed its successful position among the new universities to their complementary strengths. As the Public Orator was to say of his contribution to the early days of U.E.A. when in October 1969 an honorary degree was conferred on him, he 'brought to the offices of the first Pro Chancellor of the University and Chairman of its Council a lively sense of the vitally important role of the layman in university business in a period when the universities are being dragged more and more into the public eye and subjected to the scrutiny of an increasingly critical and often barely comprehending public'. His great achievement in this task was to ensure that U.E.A. had the wholehearted support of the county, which at the start was far from certain, for it had started as solely a City project and as such could never have succeeded.

The choice of a Chancellor was an early bone of contention. Many maintained that, especially in Norfolk, a member of the Royal Family would provide a new institution with a valuable social cachet. This Mindy strongly opposed. He believed that to make such an appointment must inevitably strengthen a traditional attitude towards the development of the University, however forward-looking such a person might well be. He believed that U.E.A. needed a man of high academic distinction, who, if possible, had also been involved in public life outside the walls of an Oxford or Cambridge college. He got his way and in 1965 wrote to Oliver Franks, later Lord Franks of Headington, who had been head of two Oxford Colleges as well as British Ambassador at Washington and Chairman of Lloyds Bank, inviting him to be the first Chancellor of U.E.A. Franks accepted, proving by his many years in office that Mindy had made a wise and ideal choice.

Mindy was a superb Chairman of Council. He had read and mastered all the necessary papers before a meeting and had previously spent at least half an hour with the Vice Chancellor discussing possible difficulties which might arise. He had a remarkable gift of cutting right through to the heart of a problem and seeing where the solution lay. In spite of holding strong views on many of the subjects to be discussed, he was invariably courteous in debate, though at times he found it hard to suffer fools or woolly speakers gladly. As he later in his life wrote to the then Dean of Norwich: 'The main thing is to avoid the same people doing most of the talking ... After nine years as Chairman of the Council of U.E.A. one always suffered from the same people arguing one moment that black was white and the next that white was black with equal clarity and facility.' Only in later years did he fail to understand that he must work through committees. When the post of Chairman of the Norwich Arts Council fell vacant he knew the right man and thought that he could nominate him. As an autocrat in the best sense of the word it was irritating to be prevented from making swift decisions, especially when he was usually right in his judgement.

Inevitably unpleasant decisions had to be made from time to time and it was then that Mindy's courage never failed him and he was able to stand firm in support of his Vice Chancellor. He had no doubt that if a don was not doing a worthwhile job he must be dismissed, however harsh this might appear. It was, at least, easier to remove a man then than it is today. Possibly the sternest test of his courage came with the accepted need to change the official architect to the University. Mindy was in no way influenced by his personal lack of sympathy for the earliest buildings; in fact he was fascinated by the personality of the architect. It was on a question regarded by Mindy as fundamental that he stood firm. He always found architects difficult to control but he insisted that they were the servants of the employing body, never its master.

The late 60s and early 70s were the years of student unrest. Student riots in Paris in 1968 were echoed in most English universities and U.E.A. was no exception. Mindy had always been anxious to establish as close a relationship as was possible with the student body and from time to time some of them would come to Raveningham so that he could learn at first hand what they hoped to gain from student life. It was yet another example of his insatiable curiosity about people. He always believed that in due course there would be a swing of the pendulum away from extreme views and rejection of authority. At the same time he was not prepared to allow the University to be run by the students or by those younger dons, who held very pronounced left-wing opinions. These he regarded as the more serious threat to the University. Writing in June 1968 to Frank Thistlethwaite he said: 'I thought the statement from the Vice Chancellors was first class, fair, receptive to reasonable changes but firm in respect of the "Wreckers". Edward Boyle to whom I have just been talking is very pleased with it. I gather he gave the Vice Chancellor of Nottingham lunch, who referred to the out and outers as "Satan bedecked as the Messiah", no bad description. I have always felt that the student problem is easier to solve than that of the disloyal junior academic staff, which is a much more difficult hurdle to surmount. I think your Vice Chancellors' committee will have to tackle that one – as you may well have done already. Public statements on that will be much more difficult if not impossible!'

During these years of great difficulty U.E.A. gained immeasurably from a Chairman of Council who presided over critical meetings with steadfast determination not to allow the destruction of the values for which the University stood. In this he was strongly supported by the then Bishop of Norwich, Launcelot Fleming. As a former don and a man who enjoyed fostering friendly relations between himself and the students, he was helpful in trying to persuade more traditionally-minded members of the Council that the oddly clothed and unkempt students were, for the most part, well-disposed but perplexed young people and not barbarians threatening the walls of Rome. At this time the front door bell at Raveningham rang and Nicholas answered it. A man, apparently a senior student or, more probably, a junior don, handed in a letter asking that it be given to Mindy. When Mindy opened it he found the abrupt suggestion: 'When the Vice Chancellor decides to resign may I humbly suggest that you do likewise'. Mindy's reaction was a chuckle and pride that at least what he was doing to help maintain sane discipline was getting through to University grass roots.

Following Ian Smith's Unilateral Declaration of Independence in 1965 the media and politically-minded students became protagonists in attacking or defending the reactions of the British government to the situation. With the growth of student unrest the courageous attempt by Sir Humphrey Gibbs to remain Governor of Rhodesia became associated in the minds of left-wing students with the maintenance of 'colonial' rule, which they felt should disappear. Nothing could have been wider of the mark, as Bishop Fleming was later able to explain in an article which editors of the student magazine agreed to print. Gibbs opposed apartheid in any form and was infinitely more sympathetic to the African cause than many students believed or understood.

Matters came to a head in 1969 in U.E.A. when the University proposed to award an Honorary Degree to Gibbs for his steadfast upholding of the rights of the Sovereign whom he represented. Once this became known a big student demonstration was planned to wreck the ceremony. By a complete coincidence the award to Mindy of the Honorary Degree of Doctor of Civil Law had been arranged to take place in the same ceremony. The authorities tried to avoid trouble by secretly moving the ceremony to the City Guildhall. News of this leaked out and a hostile demonstration began as Gibbs with Mindy emerged from the building. 'Smile, Humphrey. Wave to them!', was Mindy's urgent advice. The President of the Student Union should have attended the degree ceremony but was not allowed to do so by his members. It was known that he would like to meet Gibbs and Lord Franks asked Mindy if he was prepared to invite him to Raveningham. This Mindy did and the President and his girl friend arrived for tea. Priscilla discovered that no student in the demonstration had ever been in any part of Africa and the easy talk over tea was on every possible subject with very little on Rhodesia.

In 1973 Mindy reached the age of seventy and as with many of his other official positions he believed that he should retire. He had himself proposed a standing order of Council that lay members should retire at seventy. Out of courtesy and respect for Lord Adrian who was well over seventy, he deferred introducing this standing order until Lord Adrian had retired. Mindy's own retirement was the first to come under his own rule. It had been a peculiarly exacting task in the years during which he had held office. At the dinner which was given to that year's honorary graduands his praises were sung and the thanks of the University expressed. In his reply he entertainingly described his own unworthiness as a Pro Chancellor. He was merely 'a corpulent, ageing baronet ... a man of no academic distinction, who was performing positively his last function as an official of the University'. Admittedly he was the possessor of an Honorary Degree, 'the obtaining of which involved no examination nor any vestige or possibility of a nervous breakdown, yet was greatly prized!' He went on to answer with great wisdom the question 'inevitably asked by each succeeding generation, "Is it age and experience that counts?"' He told his audience that the modern world is

9a. Mindy as Lieutenant-Colonel in 1941

9b. Sir Humphrey Gibbs, Mindy's close friend and last Governor of Rhodesia, on a visit to London after UDI

9c. Mindy's five children, from left to right, Sarah, Lavinia, Nicholas, Joanna and Elizabeth, at Raveningham

10a. As Lord Lieutenant at the presentation of medals, 1964

10b. Two Honorary Colonels of the Suffolk and Norfolk Yeomanry: King Olav of Norway and Mindy

11a. Mindy in academic context: with
Professor Frank Thistlethwaite, first Vice-Chancellor of
the University of East Anglia

11b. Mindy at Norwich Cathedral: with Percy Mark Herbert, Bishop of
Norwich (centre) and the Archbishop of York after a diocesan service,
September 1953

12a. Mason David Holgate at work on a gargoyle of Mindy's head, eighty feet above ground level on the north wall of the presbytery of Norwich Cathedral

12b & c. Inspecting the roof of Norwich Cathedral: because Mindy was unable to climb the stairs, he was hoisted up in a builders' crane cradle. He came down with something of a bump

13. With the Chief Scout having been presented with the Silver Wolf

14a. Mindy as farmer: with a member of the Red-and-White Friesians Society at a meeting at Raveningham

14b. Relaxing at Raveningham immediately after his retirement from the Lord Lieutenancy

15a. Priscilla, the enthusiastic gardener, with a prize lily

15b. Part of her garden at Raveningham

16a. A family group at Raveningham, assembled to celebrate Mindy's mother's 90th birthday

16b. The next generation: Nicholas and Susan with a youthful Henry Hickman Bacon

concerned with electronics, computers and the like. 'In this age
experience is a positive deterrent. Imagination, energy and drive
are needed – none of them attributes of age.' When four years
earlier Mindy had received his Honorary Doctorate of Civil Law,
the Vice Chancellor wrote personally to him: 'You ought to
know in what very high esteem you are held here. Admiration,
thankfulness, affection are the words which most readily come to
mind when your colleagues think of your contribution as Pro
Chancellor. What *I* should have done without you these last years
I don't like to think.' One permanent memento of Mindy's work
for U.E.A. is possessed by the University. Sir Nicholas Bacon,
Lord Keeper of the Great Seal to Queen Elizabeth I, is credited
with having made three silver gilt cups from the Great Seal when
he relinquished office. They were made for his manors of
Gorhambury, Redgrave and Stiffkey. Of the original cups one is
in the British Museum, one in private hands, though not with a
member of the family, and the third has never been traced. Mindy
presented a replica of the Stiffkey cup to the University.

NORWICH CATHEDRAL

For twenty-three years between 1956 and 1979 Mindy held the
ancient office of High Steward of Norwich Cathedral. As with
his other voluntary work, he only accepted office on the clear
understanding that he did the work properly and was no mere
figurehead. To him this usually meant that in the last resort he
was in charge. Towards the end of his time as High Steward he
put down on paper for the benefit of another cathedral what he
thought that position should involve.

> The office of High Steward of Norwich Cathedral goes back
> to the Reformation. I do not know whether in the Cathedral
> archives there is any inkling given as to what early High
> Stewards did. I imagine probably they did nothing and left
> everything to the Steward, who did all the work for little
> pay. It must be remembered that the High Steward of
> Norwich Cathedral is an office of profit. He is paid £6.13.4d
> per annum and this has endured over the past four centuries.
> [In a television interview he once called this 'the longest pay

pause in history'.] I reckon that, comparing this payment
with that of a shepherd who, we know, used to receive
£2 p.a. in the middle 1500's, and who now, I suppose, gets
£60 per week, if the salary kept pace with inflation, not of
course with the work involved, then one would be receiving
somewhere in the neighbourhood of £9,000–£10,000 a
year.

The recent High Stewards of Norwich Cathedral, to my
knowledge, had not done anything until Lord Hastings was
appointed, I think in the 1940's. Urged by Bishop Holland,
who was then Dean, he recruited round him a team of
prominent individuals who made themselves responsible for
the maintenance of the fabric. The sums they asked for in
the early days were trifling, mainly because no proper survey
of the Cathedral had been made and nobody had the slightest
idea as to what was really needed. The awful truth came out
much later on. My predecessor, Lord Hastings, used to say
'there was little purpose in embellishing the interior of a
cathedral if one did not take the elementary precaution of
keeping the rain and the wind out first'. Eventually a High
Steward's Committee was formed [by Mindy]. It consisted
of prominent people in the Diocese concerned with industry
and commerce, or with special aptitudes for the maintenance
of old buildings. It also consisted, and this is absolutely vital
for its success, of the whole of the Chapter, the Dean and
his three Canons. [Mindy did not here add that, having
fostered a very close relationship with the Dean and Chapter,
his Committee had ultimate authority over them. Nor,
surprisingly, did he add the name of the Lord Mayor and
High Sheriff whom he considered essential links with the
City and County.]

It is desirable that the High Steward should have a sound
knowledge of finance, be able to lead people along, and have
a real interest in the beauties of an ancient building. He need
not be an expert architect but he has got to be a strong
enough character sometimes to keep architects in order. As
a profession I find them by far the most difficult to deal
with, as they never seem to keep either to their estimates or
to their timetables and the High Steward has got to be tough

on occasions. It is not necessary that he should have a firm knowledge of the Book of Habbakuk, that is for the Dean and Chapter and, if I may say so, that is the difference between the two.

The work involved is what the High Steward likes to make it. He will be regarded with suspicion by the Chapter at first, unless he has the Dean with him in the earlier stages. He will also be treated with suspicion by the Cathedral architects and that is a very good thing ... He should be a good picker of people. If he has got a good High Steward's Committee, who are prepared to work with him, then life is relatively easy.

From this specification it is clear that the office of High Steward was a task tailor-made for Mindy. Right at the start he was determined to have no more appeals for money. There had been one in 1950 'for a ridiculous figure, some £20,000, which they said they needed to maintain the building for fifteen years and which we found extremely difficult to get. People are absolutely fed up with appeals and there has not been an appeal for 25 years'. Instead, the Friends of the Cathedral, a body with whom the High Steward's committee worked in close accord, promised to become responsible for meeting the cost of maintaining the fabric of the building. This was inevitably a never-ending task for a nine hundred years old building must always need care and protection. To control this Mindy insisted on the architects furnishing his committee with a 'rolling programme' of essential work each year. But the urgent need for full-scale restoration to repair the ravages of previous years of neglect was a daunting task. Mindy's aim was to hand over to future generations a completely restored Cathedral in the hope that the maintenance of a continuous rolling programme of work would ensure that what had been put right would not again be allowed to fall into decay. In the course of a quarter of a century over half a million pounds were raised and spent, justifying his proud claim that 'more has been done to this building in the last 25 years than since it was built ... I think we could say that Norwich Cathedral is in as good repair now as any other cathedral in the country'.

That claim concealed the extent of what needed to be done. In all, some two acres of roofs, covering the nave, the north and south transepts, the presbytery and the east walk of the cloisters, were removed and replaced. Although reinforced concrete with a lead covering was used, oak timbers were also needed. With great foresight, five years before they were needed, Mindy had persuaded Norfolk landowners to fell and donate to the Cathedral ninety oak trees, so that, duly seasoned, the timber was ready to be sawn into rafters. When the rafters were finished and in place all the craftsmen and their families were entertained to a celebration at Raveningham and later the names of those who had given the oaks were recorded in the Cathedral.

In the course of the work on the roofs Mindy fell foul of the conservationists, who protested strongly at his not having insisted on the replacement of the original timbers. So he went to the builders' yard and explained the problem to the foreman, who gave him a random piece of the old roofs: 'That is why we couldn't put it back.' The wood was quite rotten and damp like a sponge. Mindy packed it up and sent it to Lord Grafton, who had led the protest. Mindy had another answer to the conservationists. One aisle had been restored by using such of the existing old timber as was still sound: the other aisle had the new timber. By doing this, under the existing Value Added Tax laws, he found that he could save the Cathedral about £30,000. The conservationists then maintained that what Mindy had allowed to be done in the Cathedral would lead those in charge of church buildings to strip their roofs to avoid payment of V.A.T.

The most alarming problem was to make safe the tower and its spire. The great arches of the Norman tower had never been intended to support the weight of a spire, which was not built until 1463, and they were cracking under the strain. When the Cathedral architect, Sir Bernard Feilden, inspected the inside of the spire he found the brickwork breaking away from the stone casing and that the iron ties, inserted two hundred years ago as reinforcements, had rusted until they were little thicker than wire. There was a very real danger that sonic boom from passing aircraft might lead to the collapse of tower and spire and an orchestral concert planned to be held beneath the tower was cancelled as a precaution. A serious but less immediate danger was posed by the lofty decorated windows in the presbytery, where the stone had become so eroded that they threatened to fall in.

The Friends of the Cathedral had made themselves responsible for covering the cost of the rolling programme; they could not have done more. It was a wonderful stroke of luck for the Cathedral when a benefactor, who in his lifetime insisted on being anonymous, came to its rescue. Mr Baron Ashe, a wealthy bachelor interested in the arts, gave a vast sum of money to the Cathedral for the work of restoration and during Ashe's lifetime even the Dean was to be kept in ignorance of the benefactor's name. Mindy had to keep Ashe closely informed of all that was being done and Ashe frequently prowled around the Cathedral with a critical eye on the efforts of architects and builders. At a later stage he was dissatisfied with the condition of the ancient throne of the Bishop at the east end of the Cathedral, high above the altar, and he gave Mindy additional money for its refurbishment. Mindy tried hard to persuade Ashe to attend the service of thanksgiving to which the Queen came but he pleaded old age as an excuse. He did, as a result of Mindy's request, agree that after his death his munificence should be recorded on a plaque in one of the chapels and this gave him pleasure.

An enterprise of such magnitude needed firm leadership and this Mindy provided. Not only did he regard the Cathedral as 'one of the greatest buildings in Europe' but his efforts to preserve it were a practical expression of his own Christian beliefs. He insisted on full reports to him of everything that was planned and of what had been completed. People did as they were told or they were apt to feel the consequences of his displeasure and he personally inspected work in progress. As a man with no head for heights and unable to climb the stairs, he bravely agreed to be hoisted aloft by a giant crane in a builders' cradle to examine the spire at close quarters. The worst part, he confessed, was to be swung in mid-air away from the building before beginning the descent. He reached ground with his normal ruddy countenance a pale green.

He found the financial incompetence of most clergy exasperating and incomprehensible; but nothing could be done about it. In his opinion he had met only one cleric of outstanding financial ability and that had been Bishop Wand of London, who 'thought like a Bank'. Deans and members of the Chapter were thankful to have a man with business experience as their High Steward. At the same time Mindy took pains to ensure that the Dean was a personal friend, as were many of the Canons. Dean Webster, later Dean of St Paul's, whose pronounced left-wing views did not always commend him to rural Norfolk, was a great admirer of Mindy and Mindy appreciated a man who claimed that he had a hundred new ideas every day and so at least some of them must be right. At meetings of the High Steward's committee the clergy had always been fully briefed beforehand and the utmost care was taken that there should be no clash between clergy and laity. The Chapter, which always turned up in full – Mindy's example of 100 per cent attendance was wisely followed by all members of the committee unless able to plead an acceptable excuse – were well aware that it was their duty to listen and to co-operate. At the same time Mindy would always defer to reasonable argument and would respond to a quiet word that what was proposed would probably not work or that those involved in a project needed more time. He took endless personal trouble to make sure before a meeting that all members of the committee fully understood what was at issue.

Architects, among whom were personal friends, were the most likely to arouse his wrath. He kept a sharp eye on the proposals for the rolling programme, concerned that they were not an excuse to keep the architects employed. He was incensed at any failure to foresee the need for major repair work or to quote too low an estimate of the cost, later making inflation the excuse for the error. 'The Committee are only too well aware of the effect of inflation!' On one occasion there was an especially stormy meeting with the architects. A large programme of refurbishment of part of the Cathdral had been agreed and started when the architects chose the moment to put forward a scheme for a roof garden on top of the nave before even the fabric had been properly reconstructed. A long remembered, salutary tempest broke over their heads. A letter written at the end of his time as High Steward shows no change in his opinion. 'The architects are running, of course, true to form. We spend quite a bit of money on having a complete survey made every five years but they always manage to discover something they have left out. We are assured that everything in the garden is lovely and there will be nothing to stop the rolling programme. However, I get absolutely exasperated by the way in which they are always changing course.'

The Cathedral clergy were not always blameless in his eyes. When in 1578 Queen Elizabeth I had visited the Cathedral a feast was given her in the North Walk of the cloisters. In 1935 it was felt to be a pleasant commemoration of the event to have the coats of arms of all those families who had entertained her painted along the cloister wall. Mindy's father, whose interest in his family history was minimal, had refused to contribute to the cost and Mindy personally paid the bill for the Bacon coat of arms. Forty years later thanks, in Mindy's opinion, to lack of supervision by both Dean and Chapter but mainly by the architects, the Bacon coat of arms was badly damaged by leaking water and had to be re-painted. So for the second time sending a cheque to the architect's firm to cover the cost, he expressed his views with admirable directness: 'I think I have a legitimate grouse against the Dean and Chapter and whoever is responsible for the maintenance of the Cathedral, that proper maintenance was not carried out and therefore the Bacon Coat of Arms was damaged. After all, my family restored that bay of the Cloister and paid for the putting up of the Coat of Arms in 1935 ... All I am saying is, I think perhaps you are a little fortunate that it was my Coat of Arms that went west. I do not think the Cathedral would have recovered a penny from anyone else ... You can thank your lucky stars that the Coat of Arms that was damaged belonged to probably the only family whose arm you could possibly twist. May I beg that in order to have no more of this nonsense, a thorough look is made at the Cloister wall to see that this does not happen again, because if it does the Friends or the Chapter will have to pay up. They won't recover it from anybody else next time.'

However, despite inevitable frustrations and difficulties the restoration of Norwich Cathedral was accomplished after a quarter of a century under Mindy's leadership and the maintenance of what had been done was entrusted to future generations. One 'extravagance' he permitted because, anonymously, he paid for it himself. The finial of the spire needed to be cleaned as part of the work of restoration but he felt that in every sense it would crown the work if the finial was gilded – a gloriously exuberant gesture.

On 11 April 1975, nearly four centuries after the visit of her ancestress, Queen Elizabeth I, Queen Elizabeth II came to the Cathedral to join in a great Act of Thanksgiving for its restoration. After the service representatives of the hundreds of Norfolk craftsmen who had worked on the fabric during twenty-five years were presented to her. It had been a magnificent achievement, due, as Dean Webster said in his sermon, 'to dogged determination, not to spectacular appeals'. Behind it all Mindy had been the relentless driving force. The thanksgiving service had been a great day in the history of the Cathedral; it was also, as Webster said in a private letter, Mindy's day.

By July 1979 Mindy had decided that the time had come for him to retire as High Steward. 'It is high time one had a change and one must remember that there are better fish in the sea than ever came out. It is time the Cathedral had a fresh mind on its affairs as I am not as energetic as I was and I always prefer to resign when people still want one to stay rather than wait until people say, "Why won't that silly old man let go?"' Knowing that he was firm in this decision, Dean Edwards was rightly anxious that Mindy's great work for the Cathedral should be commemorated in some visible form. There had been talk of embellishing one of the chapels with a painting by a first-rate modern artist and the Dean wrote to Mindy to make a suggestion about such a picture. 'To tell you the truth, I have been hoping that it could be agreed to include your portrait and that of Lady Bacon in a picture. Do not laugh or blush; that would have been perfectly normal in the Middle Ages.' Mindy's reply was characteristic: 'I would regard a portrait of myself and my wife as a complete and utter waste of money. In due course when I die and my Garter Banner is handed back to the family, as I have already told you I would deem it a great honour if a niche could be found for it in the Cathedral somewhere. I think that is quite enough with which to commemorate me and I would beg, although it is extremely kind of you to suggest it, that no personal thing is done about me at the present time.' In his will Mindy asked that his banner be hung either in the Cathedral or in Raveningham Church.

Today his Garter Banner hangs in Raveningham Church but his work for the Cathedral is commemorated in two ways: by a memorial window on the north side of the Jesus Chapel, the gift of the Friends of the Cathedral; and high on the outside north wall of the Cathedral a stonemason has carved his likeness in a gargoyle, symbolically helping to keep out the rain from the Cathedral which he had done so much to preserve.

RECOGNITION

It was not only the University and the Cathedral which officially recognized Mindy's work. Two Norfolk cities – Great Yarmouth and Norwich – conferred their highest honour on him. On 8 November 1968 he was installed as High Steward of the County Borough of Great Yarmouth as the thirtieth holder of an office which has been in continuous existence for over 440 years. It certainly has its origins well before Tudor times but the earliest records have long been lost. Choice of the right man to hold office in the sixteenth century was difficult owing to the political uncertainties of those days. Indeed three of Mindy's Tudor predecessors ended their days on the scaffold. Between 1674 and 1732 the Paston Earls of Yarmouth had a monopoly of the office; thereafter until 1835 the honour was shared between the Walpole and Townshend families. In modern times it had become the custom to honour prominent men with strong local connections and Mindy's immediate predecessor was Sir Will Spens, Master of Corpus Christi College, Cambridge, who had been Regional Civil Defence Commissioner throughout the war years.

Traditionally the new High Steward is presented with a miniature tun of wine and a silver model of a herring. These gifts followed a complaint in 1663 by the Earl of Clarendon that the Corporation had neglected to send him his annual payment of £4. A tun of wine was sent to salve his feelings and a present of herrings, marking the importance to the town of the herring fishery. The modern symbolic gifts perpetuate this early practice. The High Steward was regarded as, within the Borough, 'the real representative, as much as any subject can possibly be, of royalty itself'. In Mindy's case he was already that as Lord Lieutenant but the office of High Steward was a method whereby, if need be, the Borough could gain direct access to the Sovereign.

The Freedom of the City of Norwich dates from 1370, enabling the holder of the Freedom to enjoy a number of material benefits.

These included such advantages as the right of common pasturage of town lands, fishing in town waters, free passage over sea and river channels and the right to trade under special valuable conditions. Mindy suggested that it was now more practical to have a car parking badge and he was given one near the Castle. The Freedom was originally not too difficult to obtain as it could be gained by purchase, patrimony, apprenticeship or gift. However, this ended with the Municipal Corporation Act of 1835, designed to make local government more efficient and less corrupt. The modern procedure dates from an Act of 1885 which gave the City Council power to grant the Honorary Freedom to 'persons of distinction and any persons who have rendered eminent service to the Borough'.

It was proposed in 1977 to make two Honorary Freemen – Mindy and Sir Arthur South. The latter had given valuable service to the City but happened to be a prominent supporter of the Labour Party. It was foolishly suggested to Mindy that he might prefer not to be given the honour on the same occasion as South. His reply was characteristically blunt. Unless they were both made Freemen together he would unhesitatingly decline the honour; nor would he accept it unless the vote to award the Freedom was unanimous. So on 10 November 1977 he and Sir Arthur South became the nineteenth and twentieth recipients of the Freedom since 1885. Their comparatively few predecessors shows that the Freedom of the City of Norwich was not lightly bestowed.

Both the High Stewardship of Great Yarmouth and the Freedom of the City of Norwich were honours highly prized by Mindy. The long history of both offices appealed to him and he took justifiable pride in feeling that he was but the most recent addition to the roll of those who had served Norfolk over the centuries.

10

The Price of Duty

In recounting all that Mindy did for Norfolk and beyond it is important to realize that during the last twenty-five years of his life, the time during which he was at his most active, he was far from being a really fit man. Heavily built, he paid a heavy price for the demands which his ceaseless activity made upon his health. In the year before his marriage he had taken medical advice about how best to lose weight but it was not until April 1958 that the strain took its toll.

Needing to catch an early train next morning in order to attend meetings in Norwich, he spent the night following a Yeomanry dinner in the Liverpool Street hotel rather than at his club. During the night he suffered a very serious coronary attack. Having a shrewd idea of what was happening to him, he was able to reach the bedside telephone and ring for help. He was immediately taken to St Bartholomew's Hospital where it was thought unlikely that he would survive. Priscilla, who had been summoned to come at once, scarcely left the hospital during the two weeks in which he was in a critical condition. 'Barts' takes a pride in never having had private wards but at first Mindy was so ill that he was placed in the ward sister's room adjoining one of the wards. That his doctor, Sir Ronald Bodley-Scott, kept him in hospital for nine weeks shows how ill he had been.

As he slowly recovered Mindy became the life and soul of his ward, enjoying the company of Smithfield porters and the local Hackney residents, while firmly refusing to be moved to a private room in King Edward VII's Hospital for Officers. He liked being examined by medical students during the doctors' rounds of the wards and he took great interest in their hopes and prospects. Modern medicine might have enabled him to leave hospital sooner but Bodley-Scott was taking no chances with a patient who lived so far away as Norfolk. Even on his return home it was felt wise that Priscilla, who was driving him, should break the journey in Hertfordshire. Back at Raveningham he accepted that it was only sensible to obey his doctor's advice if he wanted to resume a fully active life. To a friend, who had also suffered a heart attack, he wrote, 'Implicitly obey your doctors. I presume they know their onions'. He was not allowed to do any work until October.

That Christmas Mindy's gratitude to his doctor was expressed in the gift of a large turkey. In his letter of thanks Bodley-Scott wrote: 'I hope that you and your wife will have a happy Christmas and that 1959 will be a kinder year to you both than 1958. I say "both" because I think that your illness was as much a strain on your wife – who was wonderful throughout it all – as it was on you who, of course, was equally wonderful. I am sure that you should now try and forget about doctors and past troubles.' The Christmas turkey became an annual gift throughout Bodley-Scott's life.

All went well for several years and Mindy's heart responded to his care over diet though there was no diminution of his activities. However, it was not only his heart which caused him trouble. In the late sixties he was in considerable pain from a duodenal ulcer, which, at one moment as has been told, he felt bound to disregard in order to keep his promise to fly to Rhodesia to help Sir Humphrey Gibbs. There was little doubt in his own mind, nor in that of his family, that his heavy responsibilities in 1977, the Silver Jubilee year of the Queen's reign, caused a recurrence of serious heart trouble.

During 1978 he had frequently felt very unwell and had made an appointment to see Sir Richard Bayliss, who had become his doctor after Bodley-Scott's retirement. He had arranged to meet Priscilla, who had been staying with her mother at Woodstock, at Bayliss's consulting rooms. He himself had been at the Carlton Club but on reaching Harley Street felt bound to ask the taxi driver to carry his small bag to the door. Bayliss later remarked that it was the first time in his experience that a patient had had a heart attack in his room. He at once arranged for Mindy to be taken to King Edward VII's Hospital for Officers where he remained for over a fortnight.

When he was allowed back to Raveningham an existing luggage lift was modernized so that he could avoid climbing the stairs to his bedroom. Before long it became clear that his heart disease had not been controlled. His secretary called Priscilla in from the garden where she was looking after some grandchildren. Mindy, looking ghastly, said 'I think I have had another turn'. He could not move from his chair and a gardener helped to bring a bed to the study as he could never have reached his bedroom. A thrombosis developed in his leg and for forty-eight hours he was in agony. After two nights during which she never left him and got what sleep she could on the sofa, Priscilla rang their local doctor at 7 a.m. wanting him to examine Mindy so as to report professionally to Bayliss. Eventually Bayliss advised her to get him at once to London but his secretary could find no private bed available for him. In desperation Priscilla said that she would wait no longer and asked the secretary to tell Bayliss that with her daughter, Elizabeth, she was driving Mindy straight to Westminster Hospital where Bayliss was a consultant. Here the secretary managed to book a bed for him in a ward. In retrospect Priscilla realizes that it was a rash drive but she did not wish to fuss Mindy by organizing trains and help at the stations. Somehow, she says, after two days and nights of intense anxiety, she never thought of an ambulance. Fortunately he stood the journey well and on reaching the hospital found the Dean of Gloucester in the opposite bed. He at once wanted to go over and make his acquaintance but was firmly put to bed. On the second night in hospital he had another agonizing attack and Bayliss knew that the time had come to prescribe certain drugs that he must take for the rest of his life. Later the Dean of Gloucester told Mindy that his great friend, the newly appointed Dean of Norwich, whom Mindy had not yet met, was visiting him in hospital. When he arrived he was introduced to Mindy. 'I hear you are from Norwich.' The Dean-elect was slightly nonplussed when Mindy replied, 'In fact I'm your High Steward'.

The second heart attack proved to be rather less serious than the first in 1958 but it was clear that he had been doing too much. He could not afford to take any risks. So he wisely kept in touch with Bayliss about his proposed activities. Should he attend the 1979 Garter Service or 'will I keel over on those bloody steps?' The Queen, who had always been closely concerned about his health, had wanted him to travel to and from St George's Chapel by car. Need he obey? Bayliss decided that with his dislike of being fussed, Mindy would hate to be kept in cotton wool in order to prolong his life by perhaps a year but he knew that from 1978 onwards Mindy was living on borrowed time.

Nothing speaks more eloquently of Mindy's sense of duty than his determination to keep his promised engagements, even if feeling far from well. This he could never have done without Priscilla's constant support and her readiness to subordinate her own interests entirely so as to be always at his side. It is said today in Norfolk that the whole county owes her a deep debt of gratitude for keeping him alive and active from 1958 onwards. While this is very true, it is also rather more likely that her devotion mirrored what he meant to her and to their children.

11

Lord Lieutenant 1949–78

At the start of his long period of office Mindy tried to avoid using the incorrect title of Lord Lieutenant. 'I am not a Lord. My proper title is Her Majesty's Lieutenant for Norfolk.' It was a lost cause, for it is as Lords Lieutenant that the holders of the office dating back to the reign of Henry VIII are always known. The original task of the Lieutenancy was to raise troops for the sovereign but this purpose is nowadays only perpetuated in a connection with the volunteer forces. When under a new ruling Mindy retired at the age of 75, being the first to which the rule applied – 'I do not think you want a lot of doddering old men in these offices. I think you have had enough by the times you are 75 and want to put your feet up' – he gave a summary in a newspaper interview of what the office involved.

'I think you get far more Royal visits than before. More members of the Royal Family are able to travel around now and as Lord Lieutenant you have to be on duty when they visit.' By tradition there is a close link with the magistracy, for the Lord Lieutenant, as Custos Rotulorum, presides over the local advisory committee and makes recommendations to the Lord Chancellor for new justices of the peace. Then there is the ceaseless correspondence. 'People write to you about everything under the sun. You are president or patron of a great number of societies concerned with good causes. There are always a number of appeals to sponsor or help, so you are kept pretty busy.' British Empire Medals and awards for brave conduct are presented by the Lord Lieutenant, as are awards to industry. 'You get rather few of these. I wrote and complained about it.' He complained because he felt that industrial factories in Norfolk, where the parent company was in London, were neglected. Ceremonies great and small all over the county have to be attended. 'I have had more pleasure out of opening a small playing field or village hall than ever I had opening some enormous building, which was paid for by the tax payer. I have never refused to open a village hall or playing field as long as people did what I asked them and chose a date to suit me.' No request from the Yeomanry was ever refused: it was only bazaars and sales of work that he firmly refused to open. That, he felt, was a task more appropriate to Priscilla. Especially when in London for several days each week for the British Sugar Corporation or for other meetings, the duties in Norfolk were onerous. 'But I managed to fit it all in. You can do, if you are quite adamant.' By embodying many of the best and most distinctive characteristics of his office, his background and his county, Mindy by general acclaim was for twenty-nine years an outstanding Lord Lieutenant. 'I think you can say that the job of Lord Lieutenant is really one in which you can get away with doing nothing – or you can do quite a lot.' He did more than 'a lot', always reluctant to delegate any duties to one of his Deputy Lieutenants.

It would be impossible for anyone without sufficient private means to accept the post of Lord Lieutenant. The work is almost entirely honorary. Nowadays there is help with postage and travel on official duty, but for the most part the cost of holding the office has to borne by the Lord Lieutenant. As has been said earlier, the fact that in Norfolk the Clerk to the Lieutenancy is now also Clerk to the County Council enabled Mindy at times to rely on the staff at County Hall. No personal secretarial help was provided, but official lists, invitations and plans for Royal visits could be typed and duplicated for him.

Requests to allow his name to be used in support of causes, however worthy, had to be considered with care. As the sovereign's representative it was important to ensure that the Lieutenancy was never associated with controversial matters. 'My reluctance [to agree to your request] is merely caused by something that has always been impressed upon us: to refrain from involving oneself in taking up causes that might result in a snub.' Or again: 'I do not normally accept the office of Patron of any

local society. This is because I reckon that it is for the local societies
to recruit people of influence in their own district. In addition I
am President of the Norfolk Society and it would, I feel, conflict
with my office there if I accepted association with some preservation societies who cared to ask me and not others.' Once
when approached to become a national Vice-President of the St
John's Ambulance Brigade he asked what his duties would be.
On being assured that attendance at an annual general meeting
and the printing of his name on the official notepaper were
all that were required of him, he promptly refused, perhaps
additionally influenced by memories of the bother which this
organization in its relationship with the Red Cross Society had
caused him in Norfolk. Far more trouble was caused him by
general in-fighting within St John's and when he was not well
Priscilla kept certain letters away from him and prevented
members telephoning him.

Politically, it was even more important to be, like his sovereign,
above Party. Jack Boddy, the National Secretary of the Agricultural and Allied Workers Union, who became a great admirer
of Mindy, said that he assumed that Mindy voted Conservative
but he never knew for certain. Moreover, feudal Norfolk, which
might have been expected to be a solidly Tory county, returned
Labour members to Parliament for Norwich constituencies in his
day. He himself was once asked to be a possible candidate for part
of the county and he long treasured the letter of invitation. The
chairman of the local Tory selectors wrote to say that he and his
committee had disliked all of their short-list of candidates and
were in process of drawing up a list of 'also rans'. Might they
include Mindy's name in this list? His reply must have caused
consternation among true blue party workers. He declined the
invitation, partly because he had no wish to enter Parliament but
also because he was not really certain that he was a Conservative.
If any political party label had to be attached to him he was a
Whig.

Inevitably as Lord Lieutenant and by reason of his many other
activities Mindy sat on innumerable committees which, for the
most part, he chaired. As a chairman he possessed what was
described as 'a surpassing talent for compelling procedural brevity
at meetings'. He insisted that no meeting should ever last for more

than two hours, an injunction which most members welcomed with relief but which, at U.E.A., dismayed those dons who enjoyed holding forth and were unaccustomed to having their lectures curtailed. He ensured this commendable brevity by coming to every meeting fully prepared. He could thus face a long and involved agenda, let everyone speak, extract the last necessary opinion and then sum up concisely, with sufficient guidance to arrive at the right solution.

In committee work, as elsewhere, he was helped by his phenomenal memory for people and names. Once he had met a committee member he could always thereafter greet him or her by name, often by a Christian name, and could recall particulars of an earlier meeting. However, it was not necessarily all sweetness and light in his meetings for he could be very formidable. Physically and vocally he could dominate the discussion and those opposed to his point of view sometimes found it wise not to press their arguments too strongly at the time; nor, if after private conversation he came round to their opinion, to relish their victory too openly. Yet he knew that reasoned opposition was healthy in any democratic assembly. In reply to a man who had taken strong exception to his support of Britain's entry into the E.E.C. he wrote: 'You say you cannot allow what I say to go by. One of the great advantages of this country, up to the present, has been that everybody is entitled to say what they like as long as they do not offend the laws of libel. You are entitled to say what you like; I am entitled to say what I like, even though we may disagree which we do in this case.' In practice Mindy did everything possible to avoid head-on collisions, taking immense pains to talk with a difficult committee member before the meeting and to exert his natural charm and skill in pacifying him. Yet he never shrank from taking the ultimate responsibility for decisions however unpopular.

Fortunately for him he was an excellent speaker. The demands for the right words when opening a building or after a dinner or for some important pronouncement on policy were never ending. He was probably at his best and happiest as an after-dinner speaker at a gathering such as a Yeomanry dinner, when all present were his friends. Yet whatever the occasion, like all good speakers, he knew that careful preparation was essential. 'One hour's preparation for each minute's delivery' was his recipe. Even if this was a pardonable exaggeration the surviving notes of many of his speeches testify to the trouble which he took. In Churchillian fashion the notes were written out boldly on long thin pieces of narrow white pasteboard with the key words of each successive sentence clearly marked. Important speeches were often rehearsed in his bath and in later years his grandchildren used to listen with glee at the keyhole to half-understood orations.

For Mindy to preside over the magistracy was no formality. He took great pains in the selection of the best men and women to recommend as justices of the peace. He was concerned to ensure that an exact balance between political parties was maintained on every magistrates' bench and he was especially anxious to see that working people were encouraged to share in the work of the bench. In 1974 a nation-wide re-organization of the magistracy took place. The main feature was the merging of smaller courts to form larger administrative units. This controversial closure of time-honoured courts where local worthies had sat in judgment over long years caused great anger. Never was Mindy's skill as a pacifier more in demand. Whenever possible he tried to forestall trouble by explaining to potentially disgruntled magistrates the reasons for what had been decided and those who would shortly have no court in which to dispense justice were to some extent mollified. Occasionally he had the more difficult task of asking for the resignation of an unsuitable justice and because of the personal care which he took the change was made with as little resentment as was possible in the circumstances.

The annual meeting of the Justices Advisory Committee was a great occasion. It was held each December at Raveningham and once business was concluded a Christmas lunch followed. Mindy carved the turkey and members of the family waited on the guests. Consternation arose after a letter had been received from the Lord Chancellor suggesting that June would be a better month in which to hold the annual meeting. The letter had been prompted by a Home Office representative who had been sent to sit in at the meeting and who apparently felt that such a meal provided by Mindy and Priscilla might be construed as a way of influencing the magistrates. Mindy was highly amused when Jack Boddy, the Trade Union official and one of the justices, pointed out that turkey and plum pudding should not really be eaten in June and that as the lunch party was such a happy feature of the Committee's year the Lord Chancellor's suggestion should be ignored. Mindy felt that his justices had got their priorities right and no change was made.

The most dramatic test of Mindy's leadership as Lord Lieutenant came when he had only been in office for some four years. It is not always realized that some 3,000 square miles of agricultural and over-built land in England and Wales are below high-water level and without the barriers constructed by engineers would be inundated at every high tide. Twice in every lunar month the sea water rises to its maximum height on known dates and the defences have been designed to meet any threatened danger. However, the sea is also subject to 'surges' of varying degree depending upon the barometric pressure. These surges cannot easily be predicted like the bi-monthly high tides but they are only dangerous if they coincide with an exceptionally high tide. At the end of January 1953 a great surge of between six and eight feet in the North Sea happened to coincide with the high spring tides, breaking first through the defences of Holland and on the night of 31 January/1 February with devastating effect through the defences of eastern England. It was without parallel since Tudor times.

Driven by wind, which at one time reached 113 miles per hour, the surge first hit Lincolnshire. As it moved southwards some 1,400 miles of sea and tidal embankment were affected. Breaches occurred in 1,200 places and between Yorkshire and Kent 160,000 acres were inundated, drowning people and livestock. Whereas Holland suffered more severely with the loss of 1,800 lives, in England over 300 perished, of whom 84 lived in Norfolk. Homes were smashed to pieces and it was said that Salthouse looked as if it had been hit by high explosives. In a desperate attempt to fill the gaps 9,000 troops in Eastern Command, greatly aided by American servicemen stationed in East Anglia, worked in freezing conditions. In all some 25,000 men were employed. 'Many acts of great gallantry were performed on Saturday night and Sunday morning in the badly affected areas. Many were carried out by people unknown and may never come to light', as Mindy reported. On Thursday 5 February there was renewed threat of danger. Gangs worked by oil lamps to seal the railway embankment and by morning on 6 February it was clear that the emergency defences were holding and the sea had been kept back.

On the morning of Sunday 1 February Mindy began a thorough tour of every part of the devastated county. Norfolk had borne the brunt of the flooding and his military training stood him in good stead as he energetically organized the relief work. Speed of action was essential and on 3 February he opened and headed a county relief fund. He knew that families who had lost everything needed financial help and that to be of the greatest use money should be distributed promptly. When the final figures of the national relief fund were published it showed that in proportion to the size of its population Norfolk had raised a larger sum than any other county and that nowhere else had the suffering been so swiftly relieved. As a matter of principle, Mind would never be associated with national appeals but only with those specific to Norfolk.

The floods of 1953 had made it clear that Norfolk's comparatively new Lord Lieutenant was a man of action, with a clear mind for administration and a grasp of detail, whose visits to destroyed villages and inundated farms, where the entire livestock had been lost, showed him to be a man of real compassion, whose presence had been a comfort. For years afterwards, because the sea water had reached first floor level and sometimes higher, the salt in the bricks and mortar made the affected houses very damp.

A little while later he wanted to present a piece of silver to the Mess of the American Airborne forces, who had given untiring help in the emergency. He asked Priscilla to get hold of a model of a pheasant, which would be formally presented after an inspection of the troops. On arrival he enquired of the commanding officer what his wishes about the inspection were. 'Just do the front rank. Don't bother about the rest', was the reply. Mindy promptly decided to inspect each rank with as much care as if he were inspecting a famous British regiment. Nevertheless, the silver was greatly appreciated as the American forces did not have mess silver to the same extent as British regiments.

Despite the military origins of the office, Mindy was extremely unlikely to be called upon to inspect a British regiment. There were practically no army units of the Regular forces stationed in

Norfolk and since 1921 the power of a Lord Lieutenant 'to call upon all able bodied men in the county to fight in the case of need' had been lost. Should any question of an inspection or presentation of colours arise, then he believed that 'with the considerable number of younger members of the Royal Family available to do this work' it had ceased to be, at any rate in Norfolk, the work of the Lord Lieutenant. Association with the Territorial Army was quite different and it has been seen how for Mindy no request for help from the Yeomanry was willingly turned down.

Before he retired from the Lieutenancy in 1978 he compiled some notes for the assistance of his successor, making clear that he was only describing his own practice, which in no way should bind future holders of the office. At the same time the notes provide an interesting insight into how he interpreted his duties. The constant requests to perform innumerable public duties could only be accepted or refused according to one's own sense of priorities. In Mindy's case it has been shown how much he preferred the small village occasion to more outwardly important tasks. He certainly accepted more of these requests than he should have done with the risk to his health but NAH 1, with Priscilla at the wheel and Mindy navigating, flashed all over the county often regardless of speed limits. The police were said to observe a discreet silence when they saw the number plate approaching.

On the vexed question of recommendations for honours he was crystal clear. 'Avoid this like the plague. Everybody thinks that the Lord Lieutenant is the proper vehicle through which approaches for Honours should be made. In fact quite a lot of people believe that the Lord Lieutenant has a private cache from which he can distribute to those he considers worthy. In very exceptional circumstances the Lord Lieutenant can write to 10 Downing Street and make recommendations. The chances of success are absolutely minimal ... It is much better to tell people to go either through their M.P. or direct to the Permanent Secretary of the Government Department concerned with the work of the individual.' The lesser matter of invitations to Royal garden parties was easier and could be more flexible. To fill the sixty or seventy places allotted to the county he used to concentrate on a different group of people each year. He was also ready to consider sympathetically requests from individuals for an invitation, 'if they are suitable and worthy'. He was not impressed by one couple, who came several times to church at Raveningham and gave a large donation. A great deal of work was involved each April when the lists had to be made and sent to Buckingham Palace. The Lord Lieutenant was required to provide the full names, address and status of those to be invited.

Inevitably the Lord Lieutenant had to be directly concerned with any Royal visit. It was Mindy's practice to call a meeting with City and County officials to work out the places which he would then suggest that a member of the Royal Family might visit. The police were responsible for working out the detailed timing. It is the Lord Lieutenant's duty to see that proper arrangements are made, to welcome the Royal visitor first, then to present his wife and the person most involved with the occasion. Thereafter Mindy made it a rule to stand back and join those in waiting. He was always careful not to steal the limelight, within their own cities or towns, giving precedence to the Lord Mayor or Mayor. Such people are 'in action for only one year and it is the great year of their lives, whereas we go on for very much longer'. Requests to write to invite a member of the Royal Family to take part in some paticular function needed to be handled carefully. 'One thing you must not do and that is to start at the top and gradually work your way down as you get refusals. You have got to make up your mind as to who you want, have a go and if you fail that is that.'

Of Mindy's own meetings with the Queen and other members of the Royal Family protocol makes it impossible to write with any certainty. There is, however, a good deal of indirect evidence that the Queen was fond of him, loved to hear his Norfolk stories as did the Queen Mother, and valued his judgement. He would be invited to shoot at Sandringham in the autumn and again in January when he and Priscilla would be invited to stay. What is quite certain is Mindy's high regard for the Queen. He was devoted to her as his sovereign and in her own person. His unquestioning loyalty sprang from something about which he rarely spoke – his deep-seated love of his own country.

As the representative of the sovereign he maintained the highest standards in his Lieutenancy. Rigid punctuality and minute attention to detail mattered greatly to him, though even he could not keep the Queen Mother to the prescribed timetable when she was giving such evident pleasure to all involved in her visit. One small example of his passion for accuracy of detail will suffice. In March 1976 he wrote to the editor of the *Tatler and Bystander*:

> I noticed in your March issue that a photograph of my wife and myself in the section in Town and Country, which was taken at the installation of His Royal Highness the Duke of Kent as High Steward of King's Lynn back in the autumn. If you study this picture you will see that I am shown wearing my medals on my right side instead of my left and the sash, which should be worn over my left shoulder is shown as being over my right. It is quite obvious what has happened. Some operator has got the negative the wrong way round. I do hope that your attention having been drawn to what has taken place, you will be a little more careful in future to check on the activity of your sub-editors and galley-proof checkers.

An eye for detail could avoid an awkward situation. Once when the late Princess Royal was visiting Norwich Mindy and Priscilla drove to the city with a new Lord Lieutenant's flag on the bonnet of the car. During the journey they both thought that it was flying upside down and so was a distress signal. They drew in to the side of the road and removed the flag, wrongly fixed by the flag makers to its holder. It was a moment when King George VI was seriously ill and the error, if undetected, might have distressed the Princess Royal. Later, another flag and pole were given by the makers with abject apologies.

The year 1977, the Silver Jubilee Year, was a particularly heavy one for all Lord Lieutenants. In the course of her visits to all counties the Queen visited Norfolk on 11 July. All the detailed planning had to be completed well in advance of the visit but it needed Mindy's eye for detail to avert a possible disaster. The Queen was due to sail in *Britannia* to Yarmouth, where the yacht would dock and she would land. It was Mindy, the soldier, who after a study of the tides informed the admiral in charge that *Britannia* could certainly come alongside but that there she would remain for many hours. She anchored off Lowestoft. Something of the strain of this year on Mindy is clear from a letter which he wrote in May 1978 to Sir Humphrey Gibbs. 'I am just home after a spell in hospital because owing to, I suppose, a bit of my old heart trouble, one of my legs blew up, but it has reacted to treatment very well ... I really am thankful to have finished with the Lord Lieutenancy. Twenty nine years is a long time and whatever one may do it does involve one in quite a lot of work; and, what is more, if you are not feeling particularly fit it very often forces you to take on some duty which really one should not do, but remain in bed. Silver Jubilee year has been a particularly heavy one with a lot of effort in money-raising and I think this brought about my troubles just before I was going to retire. So I spent my 75th birthday in Westminster Hospital.'

In 1970 the crowning recognition of all that he had done came when the Queen created him a Knight of the Garter, one of four appointed that year. It was an honour which not only gave great pride and pleasure to himself and his family but was warmly welcomed by the host of friends who delighted in this richly deserved reward. Some years later in an amusing letter to a fellow baronet he declared that he had always believed that Garter Knights are divided into two classes – those who cannot think why they had not been granted this honour earlier and those who cannot understand why they were ever honoured in this way at all. 'I come very much into the second category.'

On receiving his Roll of the Knights of the Garter from the Order's inception he was surprised and pleased to discover that his appointment was the only occasion on which a baronet had been thus elevated. He liked to hope that 'I may possibly have provided a little distinction, not of my making, to baronets as a whole.' Since it appeared that new baronets were no longer being part of the Honours List, actuarial computation had forecast that the last of them would disappear within a couple of centuries. 'Possibly we may appear at the Royal Show among the Rare Breeds in a little compound for all to see.'

As a Garter Knight Mindy created a precedent. Garter robes are very costly and he knew that some newly created Knights were finding it a strain on their resources to buy them. He therefore arranged with those in charge of the Order that on his death his robes would pass to them for handing on to a deserving

Knight. His example was gradually followed by other Knights.

A final comment on the award of the Garter to Mindy deserves to be recorded. It was made by one closely related to him through marriage. 'It surprised with joy in its total rightness.'

12

Credo

On the principle that a rational man's actions must in large measure be a product of his beliefs, it is important to know in what Mindy believed and to understand how far his Christian faith was reflected in much that he did. He had grown up in a home where Christianity was unquestioned and he does not appear to have had greater moments of doubt than are experienced by any thinking person. In his younger days he had derived some of his Christianity from the views – advanced for their time – of 'George' Cockin, Bishop of Bristol, and he was unusual amongst men of his generation in seeing that the Church must be courageous in its readiness to change and that to remain stationary was a recipe for lingering death.

His preferred pattern of worship on Sunday was that of his upbringing: the 1662 Book of Common Prayer, with Holy Communion at 8 a.m., followed by mattins at 11 a.m. This conventional pattern was never superficial; his was never the kind of faith sometimes derided as 'Remembrance Sunday religion'. Probably both Christianity and its consequent churchmanship appealed to him as part of the great continuity of the life of the land. He resembled his mother, who had once said: 'I would have liked to have been High Church but Daddy wouldn't have liked it.' He himself, while never a High Churchman, accepted the supreme importance of the Communion Service in worship, which he wished to be celebrated with dignity and he liked a certain amount of ritual to achieve this. When ill in bed after his first heart attack he wanted the whole Communion Service and not a truncated version of it. If in London at a week-end he made his Communion in a church like St Stephen's, Rochester Row, where the service was conducted with considerable ritual. This he appreciated but knew that it would be inappropriate for Raveningham parish church.

This love of old ways was the main reason for his love of the Prayer Book. His main charge against the Alternative Service Book was that those responsible for its introduction had altered the wording of Cranmer's Collects or substituted new ones. 'They can do anything they like except alter the Collects.' His feelings on the subject were as passionate as those expressed by Helen Hanff in her charming book *84 Charing Cross Road* when being sent a modern translation of the Bible. 'Kindly inform the Church of England they have loused up the most beautiful prose ever written.' In any service at which the Litany was used he always refused to respond 'Good Lord, deliver us' to the petition 'From lightning and tempest; from plague, pestilence and famine; from battle and murder and from sudden death'. From most of the disasters he was quite prepared to be delivered but not from sudden death, which, like most people, he regarded as a consummation devoutly to be wished and which was ultimately granted him.

Mindy had an understanding of the nature and needs of the Church and of the people of Norfolk whom it served which was unique. Over and over again when studying his life one is struck by the vivid contrast between the outwardly bluff and genial squire and the acute, independent mind ready, when convinced, for radical change. Fortunately for the Church, as in other spheres where Mindy led, feudal Norfolk in due time was prepared to follow. No man had greater skill in winning over potential opponents to accepting, however reluctantly, disturbing new ideas. After all they were his friends, they trusted him and, this side idolatry, they loved him. He might have considerable reservations about the business skills of the clergy and he used to quote with relish Bishop Herbert's dictum, 'The Norfolk Clergy are fundamentally lazy': but in long talks with those whom he respected as priests his unflagging interest in the work of others kept him abreast of contemporary Church problems. Once convinced of the wisdom of a proposal which might demand change, as with his other interests, he would back it to the full.

Bishop Launcelot Fleming had realized that the age-old parish system was inadequate to meet the needs of industry in a county which was far from being solely devoted to agriculture. To remedy this he aimed at appointing an industrial chaplain in the leading towns who, if possible, would also be vicar of a parish. Canon Michael Mann, later Bishop of Dudley and Dean of Windsor, was the first of these appointments and he did outstandingly good pioneering work in a field which seemed strange to the more traditionally minded critics. Mindy was convinced of the wisdom of this approach to meeting new needs and he raised £5,000 by persuading fellow landowners that the Bishop's idea was wise and that Mann's work would gain greatly if he could be sent on a six-month course at Harvard Business School. Since in no way could diocesan funds meet the cost, Mindy had set about making it financially possible for Mann to go.

In more private ways he acted as counsellor and friend to many clergy who sought his advice. They felt that they could safely pour out their troubles, knowing that anything said to Mindy in confidence was as secret as that governed by the seal of the confessional. One priest's gratitude was profound. 'I had been brought up as a country gentleman, loving the country, a keen naturalist and passionately devoted to shooting. Ordination and the life of a parish priest was a considerable cultural shock to this kind of upbringing, and if I was not be a divided kind of person I needed integration. Mindy's acceptance of me on both levels was critical and healing.' In 1969 Convocation had rejected the Anglican-Methodist Union scheme to the dismay of many clergy. Canon Alan Glendining had angrily tried to renounce his living and continue his ministry unpaid rather than accept his stipend from a feeble Established Church. Mindy saw Glendining and persuaded him not to act in this way as it would not achieve his desired end. At the same time it is probable that he told Bishop Fleming about the strong feelings among many of his clergy; for shortly afterwards the Bishop wrote an understanding letter to all his incumbents giving them the necessary licence to work with Methodist ministers in their area.

Mindy was always ready to listen and to give clergy who came to him wise advice but there was never any question of his interfering in diocesan affairs or appearing to usurp the position of the Bishop. He had inherited from his father the patronage of four livings. Believing that this might give him as a layman an undesirable influence over matters which were properly ecclesiastical, he surrendered three of these to the Bishop and only retained the patronage of Raveningham. Furthermore, he worked closely with two Bishops of Norwich. For him Bishop Herbert was something of a hero, in many ways his ideal; Bishop Fleming he revered for his simple integrity and humility and the close friendship between the two men was of the utmost importance in a rapidly changing world in which past practices and beliefs no longer went unchallenged.

It was with the revolutionary proposal to group parishes together to be served by a team ministry that Mindy's support was most valuable, indeed almost indispensable. From personal experience he knew that the morale of the country clergy was low. None of the six parishes in the Raveningham area had had an incumbent who had remained for more than three years. Vacancies had often taken between one and three years to fill. Men came to their new parish full of zeal, only to meet with crushing disappointment and to leave determined to avoid rural work in the future. With so many of their traditional duties now taken over by the State, bewildered and frustrated clergy felt unwanted and irrelevant in a changed world. To a large extent the situation was aggravated by the changing nature of village life. Young men were leaving the land to find work in the towns and the bigger houses, once the homes of leaders of village life, were being occupied by new owners, who regarded them as a week-end retreat from the pressures of City life.

Faced with nine parishes in West Norfolk without an incumbent, Bishop Fleming decided that he had no alternative but to adopt the idea of group ministries, which had originated in the Lincoln diocese in 1949 and about which an account of the first ten years of the scheme was published in 1960. The grouping together of half a dozen and more parishes to be served by a rector as team leader, with perhaps three or four other clergy under him, was not immediately popular. As Mindy wrote many years later to Dean Edwards: 'We had considerable difficulty in getting the parishes to accept the group because they wanted to have their own parson, but when they were told that, if they did, they would have to put their hands in their pockets to pay him a reasonable stipend they agreed to the inevitable.'

To have won the strong support of the Lord Lieutenant and, perhaps thanks partly to his advice, of the Queen at Sandringham, the Bishop felt encouraged to go ahead. The Raveningham group was the second to be formed, consisting at first of six parishes and gradually expanding to include eleven. Not all the parishes were on the Raveningham estate but Mindy's example won over neighbouring areas and enabled 'his' clergy to be received in a parish with no incumbent more easily than might have been expected. Clergy already on the team could undertake pastoral work in a vacant parish until the parishioners had agreed to join the group. Then together a search could be made for a new member of the team ministry. The Raveningham group was particularly well served by its priests and may have excited some envy. The first rector, Canon Alan Glendining, had gained experience of group ministries in the Lincoln diocese and he was followed by the Revd James Cummins and then by the Revd Julian Barker. Between them they ensured that the people in their area were well cared for pastorally and that there would be a readiness to experiment with new ideas. The group was the first to start the training of local priests locally and it became a recognized area of ecumenical experiment with a deaconness, who acted as virtual vicar of three parishes, and a Methodist minister was a member of the team.

As patron of the Raveningham living Mindy supported the venture wholeheartedly. Although churchwarden at Raveningham he refrained from taking a leading part in formal debate about group policy, aware that if he came to a meeting others might wait to hear what he had to say and then assent too easily. Glendining later wrote: 'In the group some of our ideas were certainly losers. I guess Mindy regarded our mistakes with rueful amusement and sympathy. He would listen to lots of our "shop" with apparently the same interest as he gave to the shop of politics and business and particularly of the county and its people. In most fields such conversation seemed to revolve less about technicalities than about the people involved in them. Oddly enough the end of this was not gossip but a kind of short cut to arriving at a sensible assessment of a situation. He accepted us as we were and encouraged our best intentions.' By contrast, meetings of the

Raveningham Parochial Church Council took place in his study. Here he did not hesitate to express his views, which usually prevailed but chiefly because they were right.

It was the joint idea of Glendining and 'the two James' – Canon James Gilchrist and the Revd James Cummins – to hold an annual dinner for the churchwardens in the group parishes in recognition of their work for the church. Husbands or wives of the church-wardens were not invited. A speaker such as the Bishop or Dean would be invited to talk at the end of the meal. As the number of parishes in the group increased the number of churchwardens outgrew the accommodation available in Glendining's vicarage and the annual supper was held at the Hall. Mindy and Priscilla simply handed over their kitchen and dining room to those in charge: Mindy attended as churchwarden; Priscilla only came when pressed to do so, claiming that she was not eligible to join the party. Neither assumed the role of host and hostess.

Once when on holiday in France Canon James Gilchrist had been much impressed by the idea of a 'Eucharist picnic', which he had witnessed, and it was decided to follow this example in the Raveningham group. Mindy and Priscilla therefore welcomed some two or three hundred parishioners of all ages into the Hall garden each August and allowed them to wander at will. The party ended with a Eucharist, for which an altar had been erected, and hymns were sung to the accompaniment of a band. Raven-ingham was, said Glendining, 'a much-visited Group, mainly because we had the good fortune to be a happy one and, thanks to the attractions of the work, a rather gifted one, and also because we had plenty of people who were ready to put themselves out to welcome the Church's guests with overflowing hospitality'. Again it was Mindy and Priscilla who led the way in putting up visiting parties of musicians, undergraduates or theological students.

It was not always easy to make services in village churches lively in days when attendance was sparse. When Julian Barker first came to Raveningham he remembers Sundays with the Bacon family occupying the front pew on the right and six parishioners the back pew on the left. Mindy welcomed Barker's request that small congregations should sit together in the choir. Furthermore, he could enjoy the funny side of things going wrong in a service. Canon Gilchrist recalls attending Raveningham Church with a congregation of three others – a deaf lay reader, who was conducting the service, a deaf organist and the bell ringer. At the last moment the bell ringer decided not to attend, pleading insufficient preparation before coming to church. The lay reader took Gilchrist and the organist remorselessly through mattins and gave a thirty minute sermon. Mindy, guessing what might be in store, had regretted to Gilchrist his inability to be present owing to a luncheon engagement at Sandringham.

However, Mindy was not always prepared to accept without question whatever went on in Raveningham Church. Canon Gilchrist had celebrated Holy Communion there shortly after the death of the Duke of Windsor and in the course of the service had prayed for the repose of the Duke's soul and for his family. Mindy was furious. Afterwards Gilchrist was subjected to a tirade for praying for a man who had been surrounded by appalling friends and who by failing to do his duty had let the whole country down. It was a revealing example of Mindy's inability ever to forgive anyone who had put his own interests before those of the country and whom he regarded as having personally let him down as his sovereign.

Mindy's Christianity was outwardly expressed in a number of acts of service to the Church. For seven years from 1955 until 1962 he was a Church Commissioner, sitting on the important Assets Committee, then known as the Estates and Finance Committee. This, as its name implied, was in charge of all the property belonging to the Church of England and of its investments. He had been brought in to the Commission as a valuable 'all-rounder', with practical knowledge of estate management and with considerable experience in the City. When he decided to retire he felt it courteous to pay a farewell call on the Archbishop of Canterbury, Michael Ramsey, who officially had been responsible for his appointment. The Archbishop, among his many great gifts, was not an easy conversationalist. Mindy liked to relate that the brief interview went as follows:

'I am Edmund Bacon and have been one of your Church Commissioners for seven years'
    'Yes ... yes ... yes'

'I thought that I should take formal leave of you on retiring'

'Yes ... yes ... yes'

'I fear that I have gained very much more than I contributed'

'Yes ... yes ... yes'

'You must be a very busy man, so I ought to go'

'Yes ... yes ... yes'

In 1348 King Edward III had founded the Order of the Garter with its twenty-six Knights at Windsor. In the same year he had founded the College of St George with twenty-six priests, devoted to prayer and worship. Since the Garter Knights would not live permanently at Windsor provision was made for the maintenance of twenty-six poor Knights, the predecessors of the Military Knights of today, whose duty was to represent the Garter Knights at the services in St George's Chapel. Two centuries later Queen Elizabeth I required the College to add the advancement of learning to its duties of prayer and worship. Thanks to Bishop Robin Woods, with the full support of Prince Philip, the imaginative idea of renewing and re-interpreting this ancient partnership resulted in the opening of St George's House in 1966. Two Queen Anne houses close to St George's Chapel were made into a residential conference centre where leaders in widely differing walks of life could meet and discuss contemporary problems against a background of a Christian community. Here politicians, church leaders, employers and trade unionists, artists and sportsmen met for three or four days at a time to try to reach a common mind on such problems as the relations between science and religion or between employees and employers. The House with a resident warden was run by a Council, chaired by Prince Philip or the Dean of Windsor, consisting of clerical and lay representatives. Mindy became a member of the Council and found it an interesting and worthwhile body. The varied degree of expertise among the members greatly appealed to his love of learning about the interests of others.

Nearer home the supreme expression of his faith was the restoration of Norwich Cathedral. Not content with that he was also chairman of the Diocesan Board of Finance and as patron of the Raveningham living he took a close interest in parish affairs. Help towards maintaining the fabric of the parish church took the form of sending members of the estate staff to clear gutters or repair the roof. He held the view that it was wrong to give such a large donation to the church funds for this work that it would thereby relieve the rest of the parishioners of their share of responsibility. His practical service to the church, allied to a forward-looking approach to current problems, unequalled among his contemporaries, and a kindly and compassionate understanding of private troubles, ultimately sprang from a simple but deep faith.

Mindy had always been a great organizer and he delighted in arranging the form of any church service with which he was closely concerned. Every detail of Joanna's marriage service – hymns, psalm, reading and the prayers – was laid down by him and he had shown almost as keen an interest in the form which the memorial service to his father-in-law, Sir Charles Ponsonby, should take. It is therefore not surprising that as he grew older, and knowing that he was far from bearing a charmed life, he made elaborate plans for what he wished to happen after his death. He first drew these up for his executors in November 1971 and confirmed them in a letter to his solicitor seven years later. They are so characteristic of him that they deserve to be quoted at some length. Not only do they reflect his directness of approach to a problem, his lack of sentimentality and his blazing common sense but also his anxiety to spare his family unnecessary trouble or to cause them greater distress. They are the words of one who followed the known ways and practice of the church which, however critically, he loved.

(1) My body to be cremated following a *short* service at the Crematorium but with NO preceding Service. My ashes to be placed in a small casket, plain in design, made of Raveningham oak and buried in the family plot in Raveningham Churchyard. I wish to spare my wife and daughters from attending either the cremation or burial and therefore these Services will only be attended by my son and/or such sons-in-law who can conveniently attend . . .

(2) I am content that Memorial Services should be held *if*

desired at Raveningham Church, Norwich Cathedral and Corringham Church, Lincolnshire. The first and last Services primarily for those connected with the Estates and a few personal friends. ON NO ACCOUNT will addresses be given at any of these Services. The Clergy to be informed that this is a definite instruction. I deplore the practice now so prevalent of extolling one's meagre virtues and conveniently ignoring one's many vices. Normally the worse the life that has been led the longer and more flowery the address. I WILL NOT HAVE ONE.

He then asked that at any memorial service there should be two hymns: 'Praise to the Lord, the Almighty, the King of Creation' and 'Guide me, O Thou great Redeemer'. At any service in Norwich Cathedral he wanted the anthem from the Brahms's Requiem 'How lovely is thy dwelling place' and before the Blessing 'God be in my head'. The service should end with the *Nunc Dimittis*. He realized that there would be an evensong in St George's Chapel, Windsor, when his Garter banner was laid up but this was a matter for the Dean and Chapter. His final instructions stated his wish for all memorial services to be held at the same time 'to spare my family the necessity of attending more than one of them' and that there should be NO MOURNING. 'In the last resort I am prepared to do what my family want except NO addresses at any Service and everything kept short!!' He was leaving everything clear and neatly tied up 'putting my family to the least trouble, which is what I want'. When he finished the letter to his solicitor he had exactly four more years to live.

13

Family Life

'The joys of parents are secret and so are their griefs and fears.'
No truer words about the relationship between parents and children than those by Francis Bacon have been written. In attempting
to present a full portrait of Mindy it is insufficient to dwell solely
on the doings of a great public figure. How he appeared to his
children is bound to be different but is none the less important.
When young it is impossible for children to regard their parents
dispassionately or, until they are much older, to compare them
with the parents of their friends. Elizabeth, as late as her early
twenties, remembers a friend saying with awe that the Lord
Lieutenant was coming to lunch and, perhaps for the first time,
fully realizing that others saw her parents in a different light from
herself.

Of Mindy and Priscilla's five children Joanna and Lavinia were
both born before the outbreak of the Second World War, in 1937
and 1939 respectively. Elizabeth was born in 1944 and Sarah two
years after the war had ended. Not until six years later in 1953
did Priscilla give birth to a son, Nicholas. Almost a sixth member
of the family was Jenny Abbott. Her parents, a Colonial High
Court Judge and his wife, lived and worked abroad and between
the ages of 13 and 16 she shared lessons with Joanna and two
neighbours' children during term time. Holiday arrangements for
her were often vague and were left by her parents to Priscilla to
organize though Jenny did not normally remain during the school
holidays. Although never in any legal sense an adopted child, she
became part of the family life and was eventually married from

Raveningham. With her husband, Nigel Stourton, she frequently returned to Norfolk.

'He did not enter much into our lives.' This already quoted comment on Nicholas Bacon's relations with his daughters could not fairly be applied to Mindy but it would contain a germ of truth. Although never as distant and austere as his father had been, he inherited in a modified form his father's difficulty in establishing a free and easy relationship with his daughters in their early years. He was very far from being a modern parent and, unlike many fathers today, he was never wax in his daughters' hands. His father's Victorian attitude towards his family inevitably influenced him. It is not easy to make any firm pronouncement upon how far Mindy's apparent lack of involvement with his young daughters sprang from his own over-busy life or from some deeper lack of rapport. That he was extremely fond of them and they of him is beyond question but it would appear that he at first found his daughters harder to understand than he found his son. The experience of growing up with five sisters did not seem to have given him the necessary insight.

As a result, the early upbringing of their daughters was largely left to Priscilla. For Joanna and Lavinia Mindy was at first a tall figure in uniform, who appeared intermittently in their lives. All four girls were taught the elements of reading and writing by Priscilla. She taught Joanna, who could read by the age of four, by the 'cat–mat' system but she joined the P.N.E.U. realizing, as she said, that the method successful with Joanna led, with Lavinia, to blows.

Mindy largely left it to Priscilla to decide all questions about such formal education as the girls received. She herself belonged to a generation in which the education of girls was seldom regarded as being as important as that of boys and neither she nor Mindy was alive to the possibilities opening up to well-educated women in the post-war world. As a governor of Southover Manor School at Lewes she sent Joanna there but she never really settled happily and returned to Raveningham to do lessons there. Elizabeth and Lavinia went to Heathfield, near Ascot, and Sarah to St Mary's, Wantage. When school days were over Joanna went on a cooking and housekeeping course and her three sisters all did a secretarial training.

During the years that the girls were at school Priscilla was far readier than Mindy to take an overt interest in their education. Yet she showed a sublime disregard for a school's official clothes list. It seemed to her pointless to sew name tapes on handkerchiefs: even more she resented buying the prescribed cotton dresses and skirts, which were expensive and so bought one and had it copied in the village. She maintains that she did nothing more for her children than any mother would do but this included the burden of fetching and carrying them to and from school. Probably the most tedious journeys were those when Nicholas went to Oliver Wyatt's preparatory school, Maidwell Hall in Northamptonshire; this meant each time a round journey of some 300 miles. Fortunately for Mindy and Priscilla their daughters were at school before the days when constant visits by parents in term time and leave-out weekends had become the normal practice. Lavinia remembers how when occasionally taken out from Heathfield by them Mindy always made for nearby Eton, where he enjoyed wandering round his old haunts.

When on 17 May 1953 Nicholas was born in London, the bells in Raveningham Church rang out to celebrate the arrival of the son and heir for whom Mindy had understandably longed and had come to fear that he would never possess. Priscilla had intended to have the baby born at home but this so shocked her mother-in-law, who firmly believed that no boy could be born at Raveningham, that she yielded and came to London for the birth. She remembers Mindy coming to see her in hospital and then, after admiring his son, quickly going to Eton to put Nicholas's name on a housemaster's list before it was too late. Like many another father, without realizing it, he was about to re-live his life through that of his son. He was quite clear what he wanted for him – Eton, Trinity College Cambridge, Gray's Inn and some subsequent appropriate profession, such as a period of service in the Army or merchant banking. Remembering his own early years, he was insistent that Nicholas should have some professional qualification; it would not be sufficient to inherit Raveningham. The contrast between his plans for his son and his readiness to leave most questions about his daughters' upbringing to Priscilla could not be more marked.

Raveningham was a wonderful home in which to grow up.

The beauty of the house must have insensibly taken hold of the family, while the garden and parkland provided unlimited space in which to play safely, protected by Mindy's notices warning approaching cars to 'Beware Children and Dogs'. In the days when he was a boy, domestic help had been readily available, with nearly thirty employed in the house and garden. Long years of service reflected both Constance's friendly nature, which inspired loyalty, and the fact that alternative employment was then impossible without a satisfactory 'reference' from a previous employer. After the war the situation was very different. To 'go into service' no longer appealed to young girls, who now demanded greater freedom and the more lucrative ways of earning a living suddenly open to them. In consequence the Hall had to be run by Priscilla with the help of a few stalwart characters and a succession of frequently changing and often unskilled assistants. The smoothly-run home of Mindy's youth had disappeared for ever but his demands for continuing hospitality did not make her task easier. In the later years of his life the need to modernize the kitchen, so that it became a place in which a modern cook might be prepared to work was increasingly apparent. When they could be spared, estate workers were brought into the kitchen to carry out the much needed alterations but owing to the prior demands of the estate the work continued over five years and was never satisfactorily completed.

The Irish blood in Priscilla's veins ensured that Raveningham would be run in a gloriously inconsequential way, which resulted in much laughter and great happiness. Mindy had his frightening rages when the family knew that it was wise to keep away but these were rare and his warmth of heart and his enjoyment of a good story prevented his slightly Victorian outlook from becoming oppressive. This Victorian-Irish combination seems to have left all their children very flexible in the way that they run their lives and for this they are grateful. The story which sums up the 'Irishness' of the house is that of the fire which broke out in the morning room. Priscilla, who was out of the house, was alarmed to see two fire engines racing up the drive. She rushed after them to be greeted by the cook, Mary Bloomfield, familiarly known to the children as 'Bloomers', leaning out of the window and calling, 'Fire round at the front, ma'am, but I'm keeping cooking till it reaches me'. The story, which has perhaps grown into family legend, goes on to tell of how Geoffrey Wilson, the estate agent, was tearing down the curtains to prevent a worse blaze, while Priscilla threw them into the fire as they were very old and might be replaced by insurance. Probably apocryphal but deserving to be true.

The 'Victorian' side of the partnership is exemplified by Mindy's inherited reluctance to spend, as he thought unnecessarily, on renewing outworn furnishings, such as the morning room curtains or bedroom carpets. Fortunately, the ancient feather beds at Thonock, fatal for anyone suffering from back trouble, were not brought to Raveningham. They did not commend themselves to occasional guests but it was easier for his brother-in-law, Noel Arnold, to complain openly. At breakfast he described how he and his wife, Mindy's sister Bridget, had been almost pushed out of bed by a 'hill' in the middle of the mattress. Priscilla explained that a feather mattress was perfectly comfortable if treated properly. It was necessary for husband and wife to start in the middle and then to work their way outwards.

Mary Bloomfield was at Raveningham for over twenty years and eventually left to seek what she believed to be a more remunerative post at a mental hospital. On enquiring it proved uncongenial and she did not take the post. She returned to Raveningham but soon went to live near her parents at neighbouring Loddon. Before she left she had overlapped with a remarkable manservant called Harry Broomfield. He had once worked in a R.A.F. mess and then had become a painter at Thonock. On Priscilla's suggestion Mindy brought him to Raveningham to be transformed into a butler, cook and general mainstay of the house.

'Broomie' was a surprising choice for a man as powerfully masculine as Mindy, for in voice and posture he was effeminate. He was a great character, who had no hesitation in telling Priscilla that she had worn a particular dress too many times at official functions. Sarah, wandering into the kitchen, around which the parakeet given to him by Lavinia was often flying, could be greeted with: 'If you're looking for it, dear, I've just hung your bra on the line.' The traditional butler's decorum was not always in evidence. China tea he happily dismissed as 'Water bewitched! Tea be buggered!' On the other hand he was an excellent cook, ever ready to 'just run something up from Connie Spry', and to teach the children how to make good pastry. Towards the children he was almost a second Nanny and an constant source of entertainment with his stories or his readiness to turn endless somersaults on the lawn. Lavinia maintains that he might almost have earned a living as a turn on the music hall stage.

As a bad asthmatic 'Broomie' had a bedroom on the ground floor, with a bell at his bedside so as to summon help if necessary. He died from a heart attack and was found on the kitchen floor on the morning of a big shooting party. Despite his haphazard ways, Mindy was very fond of him. When later in the day his son-in-law, Stephen Gibbs, telephoned to commiserate with him about Broomie's death he received the very characteristic, gruff reply: 'Well, all over. But there it is.' This was no expression of indifference but showed the control which a highly emotional man needed to exercise lest his feelings ran away with him.

Priscilla certainly needed help with her growing family in their early days. Nanny Goodfellow looked after the two eldest girls until she was called up. Nanny Baldwin came to look after Nicholas. Although Mindy mildly complained that in his young days one nanny had looked after all six children and that there was more help than appeared absolutely necessary in the nursery, he agreed to Priscilla's request that there needed to be someone to look after Nicholas. To help her he interviewed on her behalf Nanny Baldwin, who lived near Norwich. She was a wonderful character whose sole disadvantage was that she was well over the age of 70 when she took charge of Nicholas. Though much loved she was growing infirm and found it difficult to make frequent journeys up and down the Raveningham staircase. 'Broomie' proved an invaluable help to her, especially at first when Nicholas needed to be carried everywhere.

There were many other stalwart characters on whom in different ways Mindy and Priscilla relied and who were part of the Raveningham scene; Martin Blaza, the estate foreman, always ready to help in the house in any emergency; Maurice Myhill, who worked in the gardens and who served for nearly 40 years; George Warnes, the forester, recently retired after 47 years' service and who told Priscilla 'Sir Edmund used to come to see me and say he'd not come to give me orders but to discuss the work that had to be done'; and Peggy Catchpole, invaluable to Priscilla both in the house and as one still at hand to help her in the gardening and to assist in dealing with the orders from London shops. A year after Mindy's death Priscilla wrote a letter expressing their gratitude. 'This gift comes as a personal bequest from my husband, who left some money to be divided between his friends, pensioners and full-time employees of Raveningham and Thonock Estates. Many of you have worked a lifetime for him and he was deeply grateful for your help, loyalty and friendship. The remarkable amount of over 1,000 working years has been contributed by you all over the last half century and the present is an appreciation of the years you have worked for him.'

With Mindy's busy life it was difficult for Priscilla to persuade him to take regular holidays. She herself tried to avoid official functions during school holidays and firmly refused to open fêtes while her children were at home. For Mindy a day's shooting or a weekend staying with relatives or friends could be arranged comparatively easily, and he regularly spent ten days every May fishing in Ireland. His business interests often took him abroad and the chairmanship of the British Sugar Corporation ensured pleasant visits to the West Indies. These were, however, often very strenuous, once involving tours of all the plantations in the West Indies and the U.S.A. in six weeks and forcing Mindy to spend a day in bed on the homeward voyage. Family holidays in the summer were not his favourite form of relaxation. His daughters were surprised when once at the seaside he actually paddled with them, up to his knees in the water. In their teens, holidays in Scotland were more usual and these he preferred as they enabled him to relive his own young days, though the lack of facilities such as hot water in some of the shooting lodges did not please him. It was on one of these Scottish holidays that Nicholas caught his first 'fish', an eel, which Mindy had to kill with a pair of scissors.

Raveningham was a very happy home but it must at times have been a rather restless house: not that a house full of lively and intelligent children is likely to be quiet for long. Mindy and Priscilla had so often to be going to some official engagement and on these occasions the noise by the front door was unforgettable. Mindy, surrounded by barking dogs, shouted for a belated Priscilla; Priscilla calling to members of the family to search for and fetch the various things which she had mislaid or forgotten. Their highly developed sense of public duty and the consequent frequent absences from home made it necessary for their children to learn to stand on their own feet as much as possible. This was no bad upbringing but their busy lives may have left insufficient time for the unhurried, individual talks about her interests, hopes and worries which any adolescent girl needs. Nor did it apparently occur to either of them that such talks were ever necessary. A little surprisingly they did not always appear to give their daughters the encouragement and support in some new project for which they hoped; but if unexpected success followed, congratulations were sincere.

There was so much that needed doing in a large house with comparatively little domestic help. Priscilla, with her tireless energy, was seldom still and expected everyone to be up and doing at all times. At any moment there could be a cry for assistance in the kitchen or a job to be done elsewhere. Joanna, who, rather more than her sisters, jealously guarded her privacy, used to hide in the attic so as to read a book undisturbed. She tells how, when she was young, Mindy helped her to advance her reading by encouraging her to read 'unsuitable' – in the literary sense – books, such as the novels of Edgar Wallace and 'Sapper'. In the years when Jenny Abbott lived at Raveningham, sharing lessons with Joanna, the two, deep in a book, were carefully oblivious to calls from downstairs.

Both remember incurring Mindy's wrath for admittedly careless behaviour after completing some task. Joanna left the lights in the pantry on all night, which was not only wasteful but, far more important, a possible encouragement to burglars. Jenny, who had left an electric iron switched on, had clearly caused a serious fire hazard and was made to write 300 lines as a punishment. These had to be in French and she was dismayed to find that 'I must not leave the electric iron on', when translated, occupied more than one line and so caused her to have to show up 600 lines.

Mindy was not, in the accepted sense, a good conversationalist: he had no small talk. His seeming lack of interest in his daughters' activities really came from an inability to communicate easily with them until they grew up. On subjects which interested him – and they were many – he would hold forth at length and he was a good listener when he felt that the person to whom he was talking had valuable information to impart. At family meals, with uproarious conversation going on around him, he would sit at the head of the table contributing with an occasional grunt. When they grew older his children had no fear of grunting back at him. Little quirks of behaviour at meals remain vivid memories: his habit at breakfast of piercing the empty shell of the boiled egg, which he had eaten, with an egg spoon, described in ancient folk lore as a method of preventing a witch from using the shell as a boat in which to sail alongside the fishing trawlers and sink them and their crew; the great sweep of his right hand as he gathered together all the crumbs surrounding him to his left hand and swallowed them as the meal ended.

There were moments when a trivial remark by one of his family, which angered him, led to an outburst. Joanna's seemingly innocent comment that her skin was fairer than that of one of her sister's led to a denunciation of her as claiming to be more beautiful and that such comparisons were very wrong. A far more explosive situation occurred which Lavinia's husband, Stephen Gibbs, who was present, has never forgotten.

A letter from the Foreign Office referring to Sir Humphrey Gibbs, which Mindy was reading at breakfast, infuriated him and he said what he thought of the writer in no uncertain terms. It so happened that a civil servant from the Foreign Office was staying at Raveningham and he unwisely confessed to being the author of the letter on behalf of his political master. Far from being embarrassed and apologizing for a *faux pas*, Mindy poured the vials of his wrath over the head of his unfortunate guest.

It would, however, be very misleading to recall only the occasions when Mindy's explosive outbursts occurred. They were memorable as a vivid contrast to his normal charm and enjoyment of life. He had, as Priscilla and the family knew well, a great gift for defusing a possibly tense situation, of restoring a sense of proportion by his common sense approach.

A friend of Elizabeth, Jeremy Whittaker, who took the photograph of Mindy in his Garter robes talking to his grandson, Jocelyn Hoare, was staying at Raveningham when late one evening a blockage occurred in the huge water tank in the attic. Water poured through two floors and Martin Blaza was hastily summoned, though long after his working hours, to deal with the emergency. All who were available helped to mop up the water and to make soaking rooms habitable. Whittaker felt that Mindy should know exactly what was happening and see for himself what damage had been done. When urged to come upstairs, Mindy's only reply was: 'What's the point? *I* can't do anything. The experts are all there.'

Far more serious was a threat in the late 'seventies by the I.R.A. Mindy and Priscilla were in London when a comparatively new secretary was justifiably alarmed by a curt telephone call. 'Is that Sir Edmund Bacon's residence?' 'Yes.' 'Tell him he's next on the list.' 'What list?' 'The I.R.A. list.' She at once got hold of Keith Morgan, the farm manger, who rang the police and also Mindy to tell him what had happened. That night the grounds were full of police and to block a possible escape route one of the drives was closed. (It has never been re-opened.) On Mindy's return next day he had a lengthy discussion with the police: he had never had any connection with Ireland; it was highly improbable that the Red Hand of Ulster, the symbol which has been borne by all baronets since 1611, would have prompted the threatened attack. The police must have been surprised at Mindy's gleeful delight to think that he had attracted the attention of the I.R.A. They enquired anxiously: 'What does Lady Bacon think of all this? Is she very worried?' Their only answer was 'I haven't the least idea. She's in London'. Some weeks later, when as Lord Lieutenant he awaited the arrival of some Royal visitor at Norwich airport, he called out to the plain clothes detectives nearby: 'You see I'm still here.' They were not particularly amused and told him that they took the matter very seriously.

As they grew up all the girls had the usual succession of boy friends. Like many a father Mindy was instinctively critical of any possible son-in-law. Young men who came to Raveningham were warmly welcomed at first but could be very quickly forbidden to return, often because of the most trivial or unwitting offences. The banning of a man, whom one of the girls had never had a thought of marrying, became a constant source of amusement among them'. With a house full at Raveningham, Mindy was apt to be uncertain about his daughters' movements. A telephone call for Elizabeth from a young man was answered by him with a promise that he would fetch her. After shouting to no avail, he returned to the telephone to say that apparently she was in Germany. On the other hand, he proudly recalled that she had not wished to see some schoolmaster, who was showing an interest in her, and that when he telephoned Mindy tactfully pretended not to know her new telephone number in London.

Of his daughters' flat life in London, where they were either following various courses to make up for what they all regarded as their inadequate education or had taken up some employment, he had no conception whatever. He assumed that they must live in a good flat in one of the better areas. Sarah knew that he would not have enjoyed coming to dinner with her if this meant finding that she lived in a basement flat and felt it wiser not to invite him. The alternative might have been a meal in a restaurant but he himself practically never dined in a London restaurant, which he regarded as a gross waste of money. Anyhow he much preferred dining with his men friends at Pratt's. However, as they grew up conversation between father and daughters became easier. Insofar as they may have been slightly in awe of him when young, this naturally ceased before long. Lavinia, who worked at the Courtauld Insitute, was in the happy position of being able to retail the gossip of the art world and to help hang or catalogue the pictures at Raveningham. She later left the Courtauld Institute to train and qualify as a social worker for Kensington and Chelsea. Although she never completed the course, because she married and went to Canada, Elizabeth started to become a barrister and at least two of the daughters followed courses for the Open University, so there was enough which interested Mindy to talk to them about and the mutual affection, which had always existed and which, like his father, he had not always found easy to express, grew with the years.

On one thing all his daughters are unanimous: their father's scrupulous fairness between them and total absence of any sign of favouritism. As they grew up each received a generous settlement to ensure that she could always be self-sufficient if unmarried and financially independent of any future husband. Mindy hated talking about money and once the settlement had been made with great care little advice was ever given and he did not greatly relish being asked. Once the girls were on an allowance Priscilla promised that she and Mindy would always pay their fare home so that they need never say that they could not afford to return. But it was largely left to his daughters to discover how money 'worked', the use of a deposit account, how best to invest money and the like. Elizabeth says that later on she got no help from her father when trying to arrange a mortgage in order to buy a house. Each daughter in turn had received an ample endowment and must now stand on her own feet. When it seemed extremely unlikely that he would ever have a son and heir, Mindy made full provision for his heir presumptive but this in no way affected the security of his daughters. It was happily to prove an unnecessary precaution.

Nicholas, as a son and a comparatively late arrival on the scene, viewed his father rather differently from his sisters. There was an obvious danger that he might be spoiled by both his parents but his sisters maintain that they took care to see that this did not happen. During the years that he was at his preparatory school and at Eton, Mindy was particularly busy and Nicholas feels that he never really got to know him until he was back at home for the longer university vacations. Although no great games player himself, Mindy was delighted that his son was in the Eton Cricket XI and was also a skilled rackets player. Long after Mindy's death, when his Eton reports were unearthed, Nicholas was amused to discover how similar they were to his own. Both father and son had only done the amount of work needed to avoid trouble; both were late developers. Between 1966 and 1969 Nicholas was a Page of Honour to the Queen and this made Mindy justly proud. He had written to the Queen humbly suggesting that as Nicholas Bacon had served Queen Elizabeth I, he would be honoured if another Nicholas Bacon could serve Queen Elizabeth II.

Mindy was determined that his only son should not be pampered. Immediately after leaving Eton Nicholas went on a two months' cruise in the *Captain Scott*, a three-masted schooner sailing in northern waters. It was a tough assignment. He was the only young man aboard who had come from an independent school. His companions came from very different backgrounds and not all had lived a blameless life: the boys from Glasgow were very homesick. Climbing to the top of the mast was a hazardous test and even more dangerous was the occasion on which Nicholas was nearly knifed but was saved by there being too many people about. Although it was Nicholas who proposed to his father that he should join this cruise, he says that Mindy had a remarkable gift for putting ideas into his head and then welcoming them as his son's brain-child.

As early as 1965 Mindy had legally made over the Raveningham estate to Nicholas. Although far too young to take charge, Mindy trained him to take an interest in it and to become acquainted with the task which he would one day inherit. But not all his careful plans for Nicholas came to fruition. Entry to Cambridge was no longer to be had for the asking: a stiff academic hurdle had to be surmounted against great competition. In view of the long association of his family with Corpus Christi College, Nicholas was entered there. Before the A-level results were known he was rejected by the Tutor for Admissions in a summary interview and dismissed with the slightly contemptuous advice that as an Etonian he would be wiser to apply to Magdalene. Mindy was furious and having no intention of pulling strings on his behalf at Trinity with the Master, 'Rab' Butler, Nicholas went to Dundee.

On leaving the university Nicholas, like his father, was uncertain of the way ahead. He spent an adventurous year travelling overland from Ghana to Calcutta and with a friend, Henry Bowring. On a later occasion he worked for a time in a kibbutz in Israel: he had intended picking dates there but ended up working in a sardine factory. Thereafter he followed his father's wish by becoming a barrister-at-law after studying, like his Tudor forbears, at Gray's Inn. When it came to choosing a profession he had no wish to practise law, nor did he share his father's love of the army, nor had he any desire to become a merchant banker. On one thing he was certain. It was important for him to preserve his independence, to live his own life and not to grow up in the shadow of a powerful father if he could avoid it. To this end he set up and managed an electronics business in Rugby. How popular this was with either his father or his mother is difficult to say but it was they who had encouraged him to stand on his own feet.

When Mindy died in 1982 Nicholas was not yet thirty; it was not easy at that age to be expected to continue all that his father had done. It mattered more to be regarded as a person in his own right rather than to attempt the impossible and become a copy of his father. Fortunately he had from 1981 the support of his young wife, Susie, a personality as strong and sensitive as her work as a professional sculptress. Although she was only to know her father-in-law for a short while, she remembers vividly the day that Nicholas brought her to Raveningham. She had come from sculpting and was in jeans and generally untidy. They arrived in the middle of a dinner party but the manner of Mindy's welcome of her and the way that she was put at ease was unforgettable.

All Mindy's family speak with affection of his love of their children, especially when they were quite young. His great height did not seem to overawe them unduly and they were happy to sit on his knee while he talked to them or read aloud – at times even being regaled with extracts from the *Farmers' Weekly*. All the grandchildren remember the sweets – particularly the 'smarties' – which he handed out to them from a jacket pocket or from a drawer in his desk. When he died it was Lavinia's son who asked Priscilla the question which was troubling him – 'but who will give us sweets now?'

Whatever criticisms may be made of Mindy's aloofness from his children's upbringing and from their varied interests and problems, to each one of them he was always the central pivot around whom a very united family, who regarded him with affection and pride, revolved.

It so happened that a short while before his death the whole family was together at Thonock, helping to sort out pictures. It was a long time since they had all been together and it was a particularly happy weekend. For most of them it was the last time that they saw him. As Elizabeth wrote: 'The tremendous sense of family that there was and still is was inspired by him.'

It can only be a matter of pure speculation to suggest that Mindy on this weekend had come to feel that his death was not far off. For over twenty years he had never been a really fit man, at time he had been very seriously ill. He must have become very tired and, except for his farm, he was finding that he was losing interest in his many commitments. He had done it all so well for so long. He used to say that if he passed the age of eighty he would be good for another ten years but he must have known that his heart would never stand the strain. Dill Randlesham, his game keeper, had died about a month before Mindy. He had been waiting for his 'Meals on Wheels', with the money beside him on the table, but when the meal was delivered he was dead. Harry Gooch, the head cowman, said that Mindy had told him that when his time came he hoped to die in the same way. His wish would be granted. On this last weekend at Thonock he had seen all his family together; his trustees had recently met; all the ends were tied up.

14

'After a happy morning'

On 30 September 1982 Mindy and Priscilla, accompanied by his consultant forester, Ted Garfitt, set out in the Land Rover to visit the Thonock woods. From time to time they got out and walked to inspect work then in progress or to discuss future plans. Mindy was in excellent spirits, for it was work which he particularly enjoyed, and they returned to Ash Villa for lunch. The second course was apple pie and when he took another helping he remarked to Garfitt, with a mischievous smile, 'I love apple pie. I know I shouldn't have some more but I am going to!' After the meal they went into the sitting-room where Mindy lay back in his usual armchair by the fireside. While resting he suddenly had a massive heart attack. An ambulance was hastily summoned and he was rushed to the intensive care unit in Lincoln hospital. On the way there he died.

At such a moment Garfitt, as an old friend of both Mindy and Priscilla, was an invaluable support. It was he who helped Priscilla to draft the announcement of Mindy's death in *The Times*: 'Suddenly, after a happy morning of forestry ...' Thanks to Mindy's explicit wishes about his funeral and any possible memorial services, Priscilla and the family were saved from having to make decisions about them. He had always hated sombre funeral services, with everyone in deep mourning, and he had loathed the carrying of the coffin up the church aisle. So on 4 October, after a cremation service attended by those according to his wishes, the whole family was present when his ashes were interred in Raveningham churchyard alongside his father's grave. Following this private ceremony a thanksgiving service was held in the church, attended by the family, members of the estate and farm and close neighbours. On 28 October a further thanksgiving service was held in St Laurence's Church, Corringham.

Next day Norwich Cathedral, which Mindy had done so much to preserve was filled almost to capacity by a vast congregation, assembled to pay tribute and to give thanks for the life of a man about whom the word 'unique' can justifiably be used. There was no one quite like him. In a rapidly changing world his work for Norfolk would continue but by other hands and in other ways. Once again the pattern of the service exactly followed his wishes, with the hymns which he had chosen and the lovely Brahms's anthem. Of the two lessons Nicholas read the first from the Book of Wisdom: 'The righteous live for evermore; their reward is also with the Lord and the care of them is with the most High.'

One further service had to be held. At evensong in St George's Chapel, Windsor, on 20 December Mindy's Garter Banner was laid up. It was a very different occasion from the other thanksgiving services. In that rich setting, steeped in history, the Military Knights bore his Banner to the altar and presented it to the Dean. The ceremony was simple and traditional, almost impersonal, yet at the same time deeply moving.

Although Mindy had deprecated the idea of any memorial to him in Norwich Cathedral, save perhaps a last resting place for his Garter Banner, if it did not remain in Raveningham Church, a new north window in the Jesus Chapel was the gift of the Friends of the Cathedral in recognition of his years as High Steward. The inscription under the window speaks of him as 'Leader and Friend'. Leader he certainly was but one who possessed that real humility which does not underestimate his own gifts and abilities. He made no pretence of hiding his talents but, as a faithful servant, used them to the full in the service of his fellow men. Friend to all who sought his help and advice he certainly was; but those most encouraged, cheered and strengthened by him would use a stronger word. 'I remember looking at the altar in Raveningham Church on the day of his funeral, thanking God and blessing Mindy for what he had done for me. Small wonder that I loved him.' An equally simple tribute came from his daughter-in-law, unaware that it would form the final sentence of this memoir: 'In every sense of the words he was a big man.'

Index